ICAEW

Business and finance

First edition September 2007

ISBN 9780 7517 4603 7

British Library Cataloguing-in-Publication Data

A catalogue record for this book is available from the British Library

Published by

BPP Learning Media Ltd, BPP House, Aldine Place, London W12 8AA

www.bpp.com/learningmedia

Printed in Great Britain by Ashford Colour Press Ltd, Gosport, Hampshire, PO13 0FW

Your learning materials, published by BPP Learning Media Ltd, are printed on paper sourced from sustainable, managed forests.

Welcome to BPP Learning Media's **Passcards for ICAEW Business and Finance**.

- They **focus on your exam** and **save you time**.
- They incorporate **diagrams** to kick start your memory.
- They follow the overall **structure** of the ICAEW Study Manuals, but BPP Learning Media's ICAEW **Passcards** are not just a condensed book. Each card has been separately designed for clear presentation. Topics are self-contained and can be grasped visually.
- ICAEW **Passcards** are still **just the right size** for pockets, briefcases and bags.
- ICAEW **Passcards** should be used in conjunction with the question plan in the front pages of the Kit. The plan identifies key questions for you to try in the Kit.

Run through the **Passcards** as often as you can during your final revision period. The day before the exam, try to go through the **Passcards** again! You will then be well on your way to passing your exams.

Good luck!

1: Introduction to business

Topic List

- Organisation and business
- Stakeholders
- Business objectives
- Mission, goals, plans and standards
- Performance measurement

This introduction to the 'business' element of the syllabus contains an overview of what a business is, who is interested in it and why, why it exists and what it sets out to do, and how the business knows whether it has succeeded.

Don't be tempted to regard this material as introductory but not examinable: the syllabus introduces the basics of many topics and the exam is there to make sure you know about them before you move on to further study of each topic.

Organisation
is a *social arrangement* for **controlled performance** of *collective goals*, which has a *boundary* separating it from its environment.
Social arrangement = structure
Collective goals = *organisational objectives*
Controlled performance = monitoring, adjustment
Boundary = identity
Why do organisations exist?
They overcome individuals' limitations
They enable individuals to specialise
They save time through joint effort
They pool knowledge and ideas
They pool expertise
They enable synergy
2 + 2 = 5
Organisational objectives
Market standing: eg market share
Innovation
Productivity
Physical and financial resources
Profitability and wealth creation
Manager performance and development
Worker performance and attitude
Social responsibility

Differences between organisations

- Ownership: private v public sector
- Control: by owners, manager or public servants
- Activity
- Orientation: profit v non-profit
- Size
- Legal status: sole trader, partnership or company
- Financing
- Technology

- Profit orientation = maximise owners' wealth
- Non-profit orientation = provide goods and services

Areas of activity of industries

Agriculture Extractive/raw materials	PRIMARY
Manufacturing Energy production Intellectual production	SECONDARY
Retailing/distribution Services	TERTIARY

Business

An organisation that is oriented towards making a profit for its owners so as to maximise their wealth, and that can be regarded as an entity separate from its owners

Stakeholders

A person or group which has a stake in the business: an interest to protect

Stakeholder	Stake	Expectation
Primary		
Owners	Capital	Return on investment – dividend and capital growth
Secondary		
Directors/managers Employees	Livelihood, careers, and reputations	Remuneration, progression, stability and equity
Customers	Continued custom	Stability, quality and equity
Suppliers	Continued custom	Stability, payment and equity
Lenders	Capital	Return on investment – interest and repayment
Government/regulators	Infrastructure, welfare and tax revenue	Equity, investment
Public at large/natural environment	Infrastructure and environment	Protection

Business objectives

- *Primary objective* — **eg** Maximisation of owners' wealth (profit)

TAKES PRECEDENCE OVER:

- *Secondary objectives* (support primary objective) — **eg**
  - Market position/share
  - Product development
  - Utilisation of technology
  - Utilisation of labour resources
  - Social responsibility

Alternative primary objectives may apply where:

- Managers lack a personal interest in wealth maximisation
- The business faces a lack of competition

↓

- Profit satisficing
- Revenue maximisation
- Multiple objectives (Drucker)
- Constraints theory (Simon)

Hierarchy of objectives

Corporate objectives of firm as a whole
TAKE PRECEDENCE OVER
Unit objectives for individual departments in the firm

Planning and control system

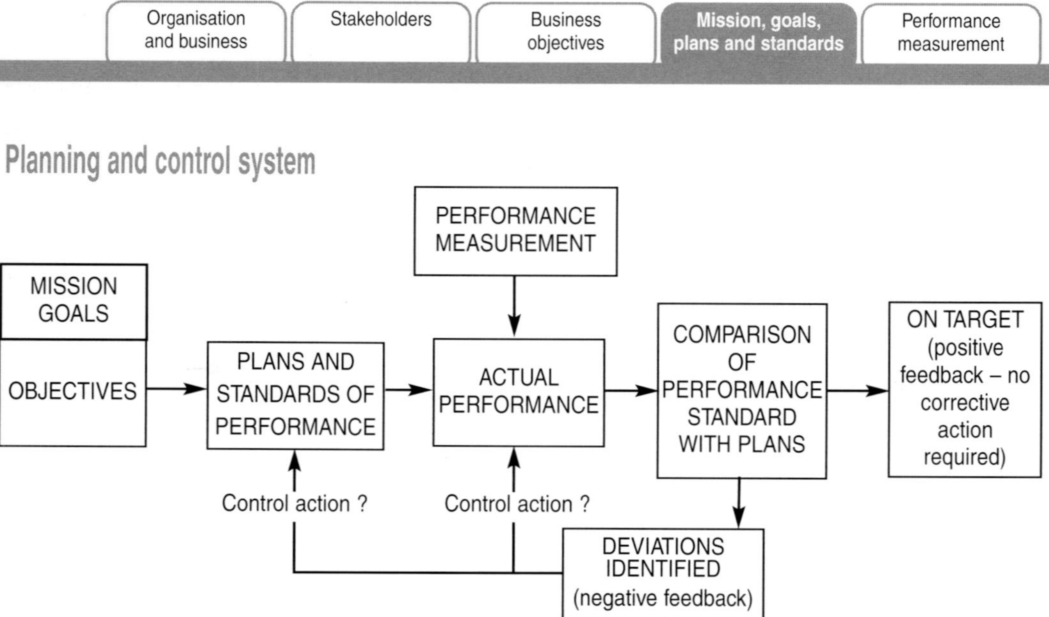

Mission

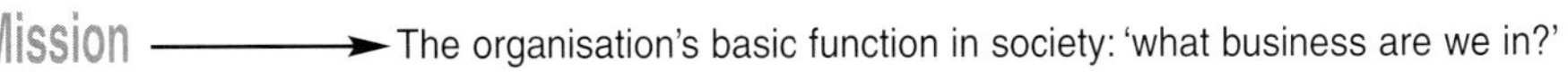

The organisation's basic function in society: 'what business are we in?'

- Purpose
- Strategy
- Policies and standards of behaviour
- Values

Goals

AIMS: non-operational, qualitative goals

OBJECTIVES: operational, quantitative goals

Why have objectives?

- To implement the mission
- To give direction and focus to staff
- A yardstick for appraising strategies
- A yardstick for controlling performance

'SMART' objectives

- **S**pecific
- **M**easurable
- **A**chievable
- **R**elevant
- **T**ime-bounded

Plans & standards

PLANS: Statements of what should be done to achieve the operational objectives

STANDARDS/TARGETS: specifications of the desired level, cost or quality of performance

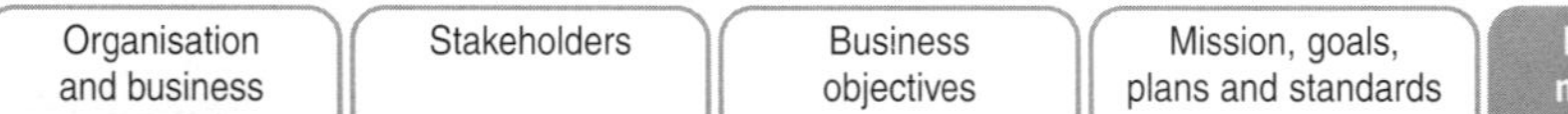

Profitability measures

Measured in items of monetary value:

	£
Revenue	X
Cost of sales	(X)
Gross profit	X
Expenses	(X)
Net profit (NP)	X

Gross profit → Gross profit/Revenue = gross margin; Gross profit/Cost of sales = mark-up

Net profit → NP/Revenue = net margin; NP/Capital = return on capital employed

Critical success factors (CSFs)

Unique to each business, a CSF is something that **must** be achieved to a certain performance standard, measured as a **key performance indicator** (KPI)

Activity and productivity measures

Measured in terms of:

- Monetary value
- Quantities
- Time

Measure resource use, and relate outputs to inputs in terms of:

Economy: reduction/ containment of cost

Effectiveness: how far target has been achieved

Efficiency

Either: achieving targets at minimum cost

Or: controlling costs without losing operational effectiveness

2: Managing a business

Topic List

- Management terms
- Being a manager
- Marketing management
- Operations and HR management
- Organisational behaviour

In this rather lengthy chapter you need to appreciate a wide variety of terms, models and theories to do with how to manage a business day-to-day.

A business normally consists of four major functions – finance, operations, marketing and human resources – the first of whom is the major focus of this exam. In this chapter however we look at the other three functions, then at how people behave within the context of the organisation.

Management

Getting things done through other people.

Authority

is the *right* of a person to ask someone else to do something and expect it to be done. Authority is conferred by the organisation.

Authority may be called 'position power' or 'legitimate power': it is power supported by the legal/rational right to exercise it

Responsibility

is the obligation a person has to fulfil a task (s)he has been given, or to exercise authority in the interests of the organisation.

Accountability

is a person's liability to be called to account for the fulfilment of tasks or the exercise of authority: in effect, reporting back.

What if authority ≠ responsibility?

- *Authority without responsibility* enables arbitrary, self-interested or irresponsible management.
- *Responsibility without authority* leads to frustration and stress.

A manager may **delegate** responsibility and authority to a subordinate to get a task done, but cannot delegate accountability for that task

Managers using different levels of authority

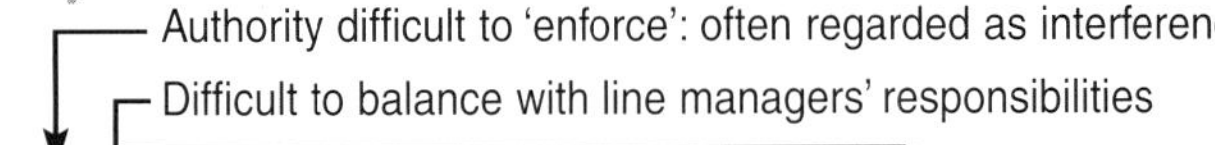

Authority difficult to 'enforce': often regarded as interference

Difficult to balance with line managers' responsibilities

Line manager

has direct authority over a subordinate in the scalar chain of command

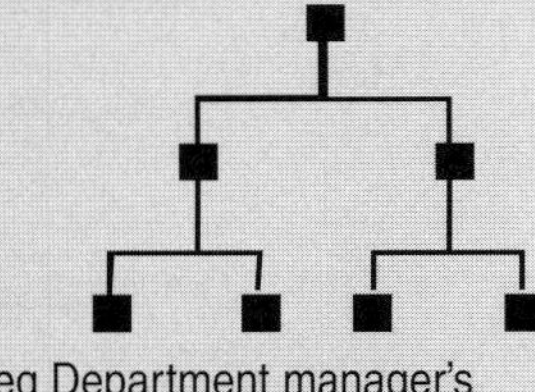

eg Department manager's authority over own staff.

Staff manager

has 'expert' influence, by which a manager or department has (limited) authority to advise another

eg An HR manager advising a department manager on selection techniques

Functional manager

has 'expert' influence formalised as authority to direct or control relevant activities in line departments

eg An HR manager introducing equal opportunity policies to which line managers must adhere

A **project manager** has temporary authority over team members in respect only of the project.

Power — the ability to get things done

Power is not necessarily conferred formally by the organisation, but can be derived (French & Raven, Charles Handy) from a number of sources of influence.

- *Coercive power* — Physical force or threat of punishment: rare in organisations, but may be seen in intimidation tactics.
- *Reward power* — Control over the rewards and resources that people value: information, pay, status, facilities and so on.
- *Position (legitimate) power* — Power associated with (and legitimised by) a formal role and position in the organisation hierarchy, *ie* 'authority'.
- *Expert power* — Control over knowledge, expertise or information that is recognised and valued by others.
- *Personal (referant) power* — Power associated with 'force of personality' or charisma - usually the result of high-level interpersonal skills (inspiring, influencing etc).
- *Negative power* — The power to cause or threaten problems, costs, disruptions or other undesirable outcomes: the only power some members of the organisation may feel they have.

The management hierarchy

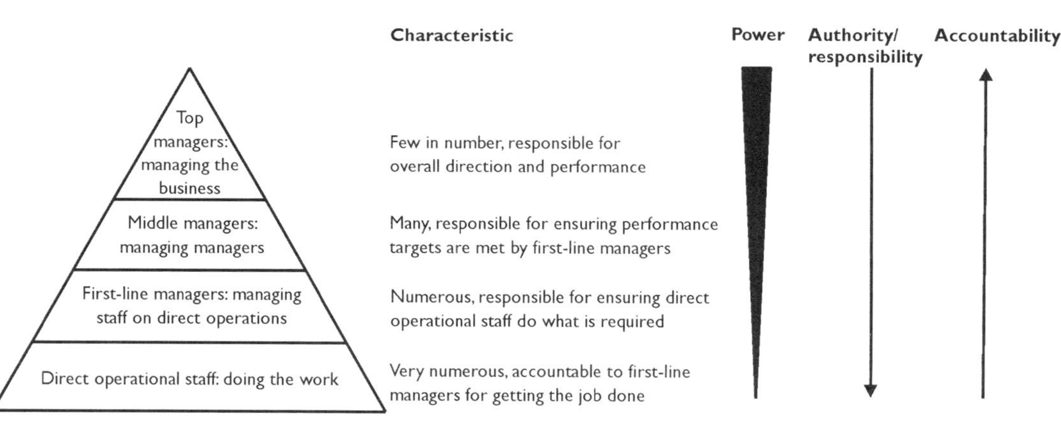

The management process

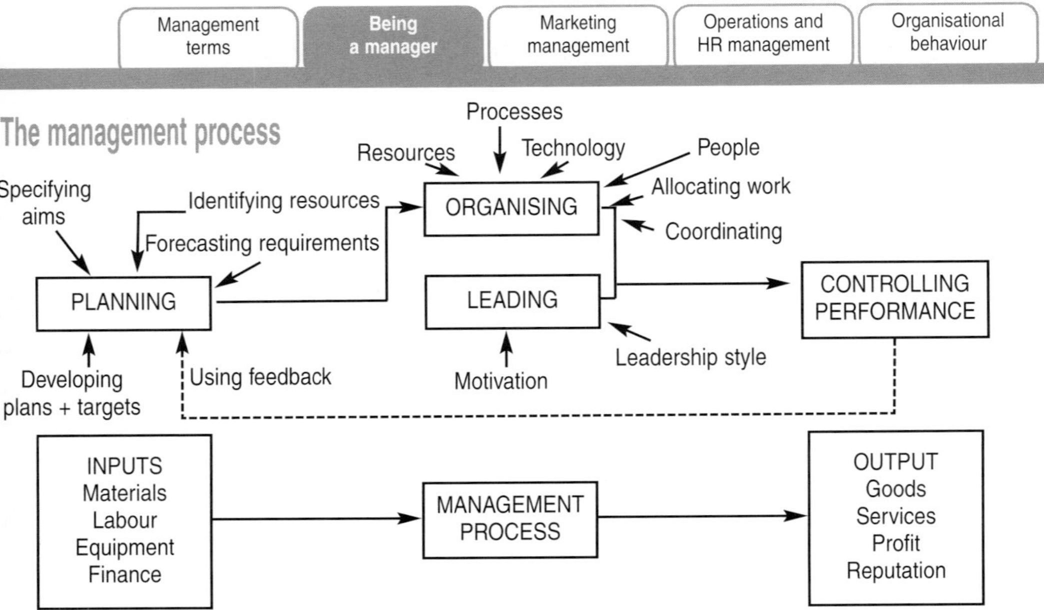

Managerial roles (Mintzberg)

Managers are not reflective, systematic planners: managerial work, in practice, is disjointed and discontinuous, and involves verbal/informal communication, intuition and judgement.

1	**INTERPERSONAL ROLES**	Figurehead	A ceremonial role, representing the organisation
		Leader	Motivating, commanding, inspiring, developing staff
		Liaison	Maintaining contacts outside the vertical chain of command
2	**INFORMATIONAL ROLES**	Monitor	Scanning for information from internal and external networks
		Spokesperson	Providing information to interested parties on behalf of the organisation
		Disseminator	Sharing information via networks with those who need it
3	**DECISIONAL ROLES**	Entrepreneur	Initiating projects, mobilising resources to meet opportunities
		Disturbance handler	Responding to pressures and problems that affect performance
		Resource allocator	Mobilising and allocating limited resources to teams/objectives
		Negotiator	Integrating different interests through bargaining processes
		Problem-solver	Resolving problems as they arise

Culture and management (Quinn)

A business's culture - 'The way we see things round here' - affects how it is managed:

- Is flexibility or tight control more important?
- Does the business look inwards or outwards?

+ FLEXIBLE

+ INWARD-LOOKING			+ OUTWARD-LOOKING
	Human relations	Open systems	
	Internal process - *how* we do things	Rational goal - *why* we do things	

+ CONTROL

- Rational, systematic work methods
- Detailed rules, procedures and division of labour
- Hierarchical lines of authority
- Impersonality and low involvement employment relations
- Centralisation of planning and control

Business functions

A manager is likely to act within one of the four main functional areas of a business.

- Marketing
- Operations
- Human resources
- Finance

Marketing

The management process which identifies, anticipates and supplies customer requirements efficiently and profitably.

Consumer markets (B2C)

- Product/services bought by individuals for their own or family use
- FMCGs: fast-moving consumer goods of low value, high volume eg bread
- Consumer durables: white and brown goods, soft goods, and services

Industrial markets (B2B)

- Raw materials and components
- Capital goods
- Supplies
- Services

Market segmentation, subdividing a market into increasingly homogeneous subgroups of customers, any subgroup can be selected as a **target market** to be met with a distinct **marketing mix.**

Target market: one or more segments selected for special attention by a company.

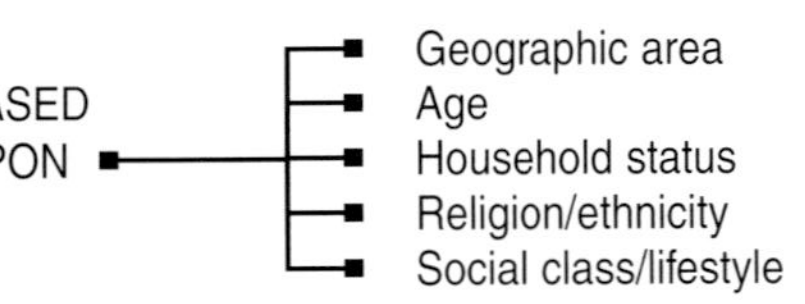

Marketing mix

The set of controllable variables and their levels that the firm uses to influence the target market. These elements are interdependent.

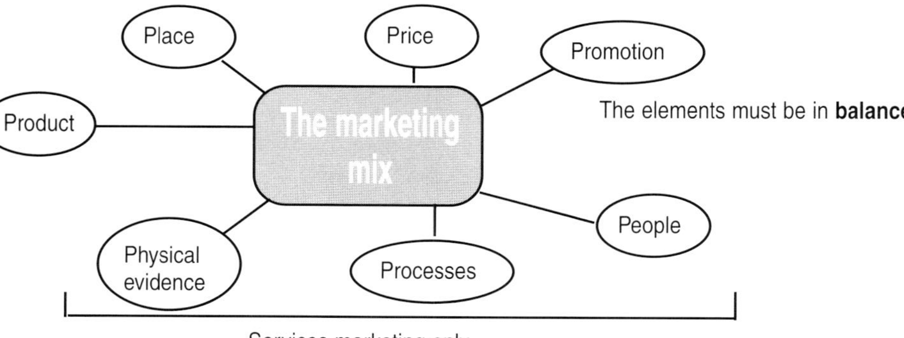

4Ps

Product

The product is a **package of benefits** that meets a need or provides a solution. The **core product** consists of the essential features; the **augmented product** provides additional benefits.

Important factors:

- quality and reliability
- aesthetics
- packaging
- product mix
- branding
- servicing

Place

Distribution (or outlets) and **logistics** support the overall marketing effort by providing the promised customer satisfactions. Important factors:

- Availability
- Location
- Timing
- Sell direct?
- Use intermediaries? (retailers, wholesalers)

Promotion

Communicating benefits to customers.

Important factors

- Advertising
- Sales promotions
- Public relations
- Personal selling
- Push or pull techniques?

Price

Pricing includes discounts and credit terms. It is influenced by costs, which must be covered, by demand and its elasticity, and by the competition. It is very closely related to promotion and brand/product image.

Services and the marketing mix – 3 extra Ps

- **People** Services depend on **people** and their skills, attitudes, behaviour, numbers, appearance and so on.
- **Processes** Services depend on **processes** and their effectiveness, economy, speed, user friendliness and so on.
- **Physical evidence** is vital and includes certificates, receipts, tickets and brochures.

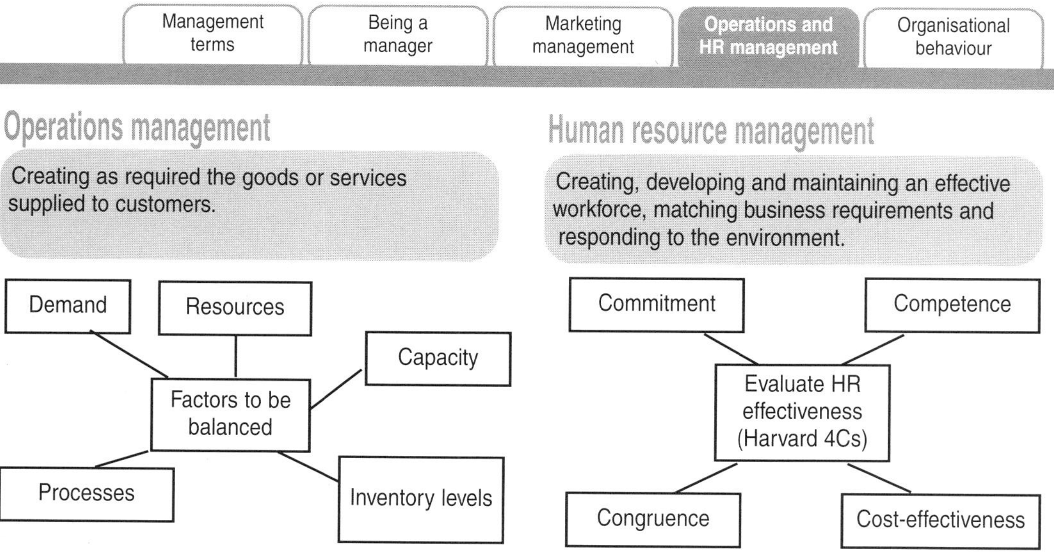

Operations management

Creating as required the goods or services supplied to customers.

Human resource management

Creating, developing and maintaining an effective workforce, matching business requirements and responding to the environment.

Functions of HRM

- Personnel planning and control
- Job design
- Recruitment & selection
- Training & development
- Performance appraisal
- Discipline employees
- Remuneration
- Grievances & disputes
- Compliance
- Communication & counselling
- Information & records
- Diversity

Organisational behaviour

Individual and group behaviour in an organisational setting

Organisational iceberg

Put forward by Hellriegel, Slocum & Woodmen

		Customers		
Formal aspects (overt)	Formal goals	Technology	Physical facilities	Organisation design
	Financial resources	Surface competencies and skills		Rules and regulations
Behavioural aspects (covert)	Attitudes Communication patterns Informal team processes Personality Conflict Political behaviour Underlying competencies and skills			

Iceberg visible above waterline

Submerged iceberg beneath waterline

Models of human behaviour

Scientific management (Taylor)

- People are rational and seek to maximise their economic gain
- People respond as individuals, not groups
- People can be treated like machines
- Main motivator = high wages
- Managers' jobs are to tell workers what to do
- Workers' jobs are to do as they are told = get paid

Theory X and Theory Y (McGregor)

THEORY X — People dislike work and responsibility. Workers must be coerced, controlled and directed in order to make them perform adequately.

NB: Two extreme assumptions - not 'types' of people

THEORY Y — The expenditure of effort in work is natural and not inherently disliked. People are capable of exercising responsibility and self-direction, being motivated by the desire for growth/achievement

Motivation

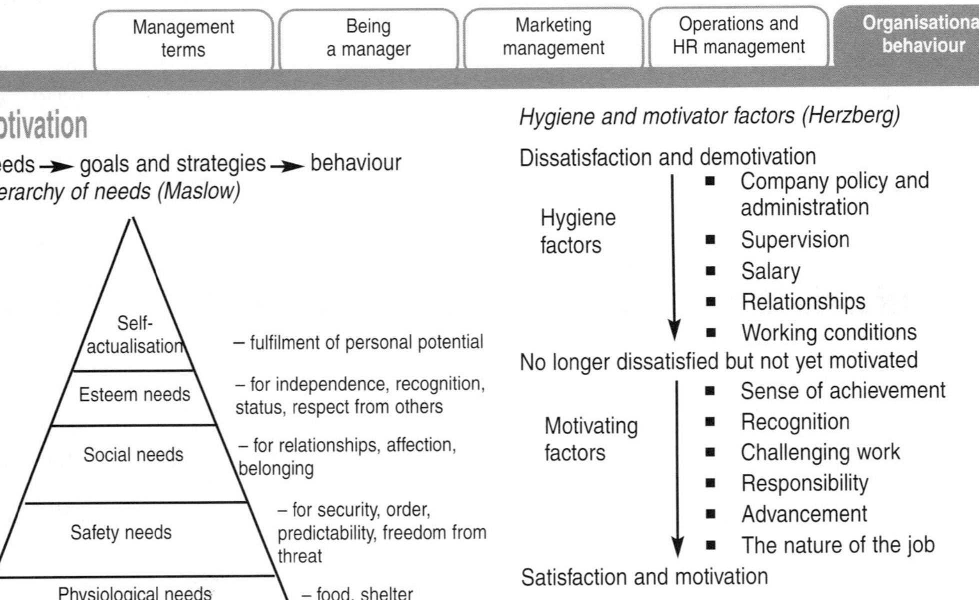

Needs → goals and strategies → behaviour
Hierarchy of needs (Maslow)
Self-actualisation
– fulfilment of personal potential
Esteem needs
– for independence, recognition, status, respect from others
Social needs
– for relationships, affection, belonging
Safety needs
– for security, order, predictability, freedom from threat
Physiological needs
– food, shelter
Hygiene and motivator factors (Herzberg)
Dissatisfaction and demotivation
Hygiene factors
Company policy and administration
Supervision
Salary
Relationships
Working conditions
No longer dissatisfied but not yet motivated
Motivating factors
Sense of achievement
Recognition
Challenging work
Responsibility
Advancement
The nature of the job
Satisfaction and motivation

Groups

Any collection of people who see themselves as a group

- Common aim or purpose
- A sense of identity
- Existence of group norms
- Internal communication
- Leadership

Usefulness of groups

For the business

- Pool skills
- Plan and organise
- Solve problems/take decisions
- Distribute information
- Co-ordinate between departments

For individuals

- Satisfy social and esteem needs
- Give support
- Provide social contact and personal relationships

Stages of group development (Tuckman)

1 **FORMING** The group is coming together. Individuals try to find out about each other and the aims and norms of the group.

2 **STORMING** Aims, procedures and roles (including leadership) begin to be hammered out through more or less open conflict.

3 **NORMING** The group begins to settle down, reaching agreements on work-sharing, roles and norms. Group decision-making begins.

4 **PERFORMING** The group is ready to set to work on its task: the process of formation no longer absorbs attention. The focus shifts to results.

Group roles (Belbin)

1. **Leader:** presides over team activity. (Balanced, disciplined, good at working through others.)
2. **Shaper:** spurs the team on to action. (Dominant, extrovert, passionate about the task.)
3. **Plant:** provides the team with ideas, proposals. (Introverted but creatively intelligent.)
4. **Evaluator:** dissects and criticises ideas: spots potential problems. (Analytically intelligent.)
5. **Resource-investigator:** accesses new contacts and resources. (Extrovert networker; not an originator.)
6. **Company worker:** translates ideas into practice, plans. (Not a leader, but an essential organiser.)
7. **Team-worker:** holds the team together, supports members. (Empathetic, diplomatic.)
8. **Finisher:** chivvies the team to attend to details/deadlines/follow-up.
9. **Specialist:** outsider

The effective manager

Influences

- Extent of authority
- Amount of automony given to subordinates
- Leadership 'style'

Participative continuum (Likert)

Exploitative – authoritative	Benevolent – authoritative → Consultative →	Participative
Decisions imposed	→ Increasing trust in subordinates' ability →	Complete trust + discussion
Motivated by threats	→ More participative motivation style →	Motivated by rewards – goals agreed
Centralised decision-making	→ Increasing delegation →	High degree of delegation
Little superior/ subordinate communication	→ Increasing communication →	Frequent communication
Superior + subordinates act as individuals – no teamwork	→ Increasing teamwork →	Superior + subordinates act as a team
Theory x	→	Theory y

Characteristics (Likert)

- Employee-centred rather than work-centred
- Has high standards but is flexible re methods
- Natural delegator; trusting
- Encourages participation

Delegation

The process whereby a superior passes to a subordinate part of his or her own responsibility and authority to make decisions.

Remember: The delegator is still *accountable* to his or her superior for the results of delegated decisions.

Advantages of delegation

- Manager freed from less important activities
- Enables relevant and speedy decision-making
- Enhances flexibility
- Makes subordinate's job more interesting
- Motivational
- Facilitates career development/succession planning

Problems of poor delegation

- Too much supervision wastes time
- Too little leads to poor performance
- 'Passing the buck'
- Only boring or impossible work is delegated
- Fear by manager of losing control
- Insufficient skills/training

3: Organisational structure and business forms

Topic List

- Principles of organisational structure
- Types of business structure
- Centralisation and decentralisation
- Tall and flat organisations
- Span of control
- Bureaucracy
- Business forms

In this chapter we cover how a business of any size is structured, and its various parts co-ordinated. We also look at the various types of legal structure that may be adopted.

Formal organisation structure links individuals in a network of reporting relationships and communication lines. It groups and allocates tasks, defines authority, and links and shapes the co-ordinated flow of work, information and resources through the organisation.

'Classical principles' (Fayol)

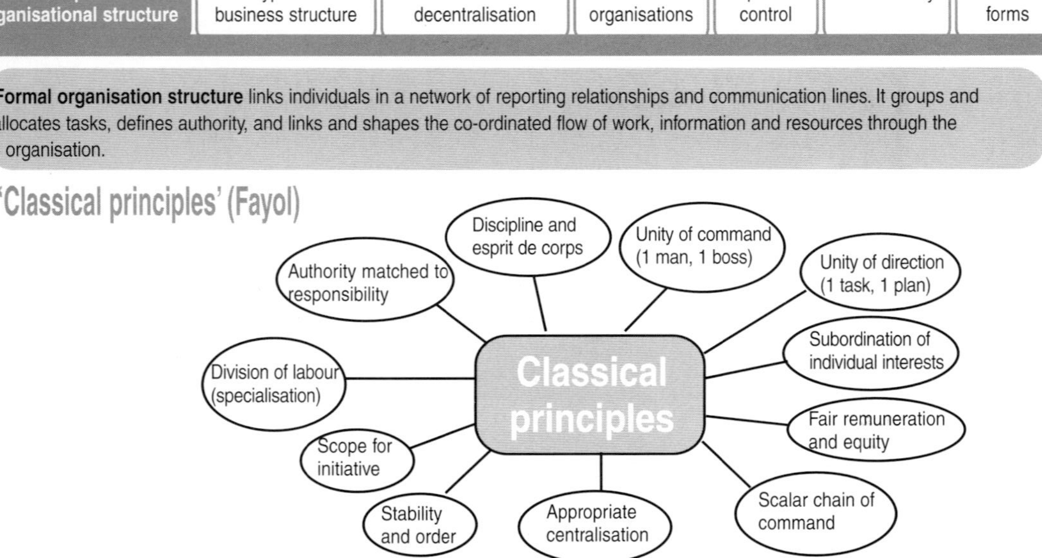

Building blocks and coordinating mechanisms (Mintzberg)

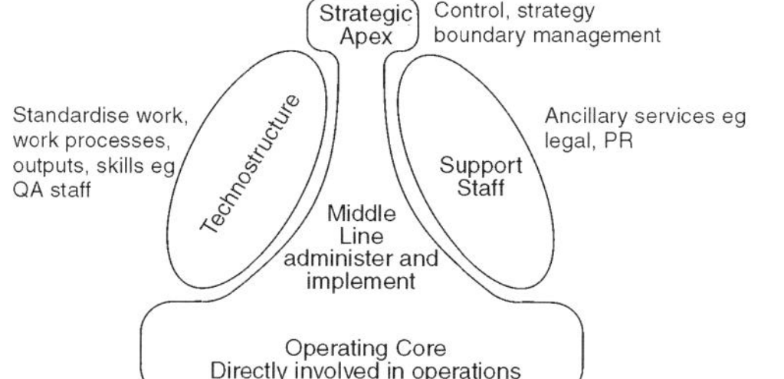

Mintzberg suggests five processes by which work is coordinated:

- Mutual adjustment
- Direct supervision
- Standardisation of work processes
- Standardisation of outputs (by performance measures)
- Standardisation of skills and knowledge

The business's external environment affects its structure

Structure environment

- Structure – slow environmental change
- Single product/market
- Simple technology
- Safe

Dynamic environment

- Dynamic – rapid, accelerating change
- Diverse – international, many products and markets
- Difficult – analysis is not easy
- Dangerous

Types of business structure	External environment	Internal factors	Key building block (monthly)	Key coordinating mechanism (monthly)
Simple entrepreneurial structure	Simple Dynamic	Small Young Simple tasks	Strategic apex	Direct supervision
Machine bureaucracy/ functional structure	Simple Static	Large Old Regulated	Technostructure	Standardisation of work
Professional bureaucracy	Complex Static	Professional Simple systems	Operating core	Standardisation of skills
Divisional structure	Simple Static Diverse	Very large Old Divisible tasks	Middle line	Standardisation of outputs
Advocacy/ innovative	Complex Dynamic	Young Complex tasks	Operating core	Mutual adjustment

1 Divisional structure

Structured according to **products** or **areas**

- [+] Local contact with customers and other stakeholders
- [+] Reduced infrastructure/costs of supply
- [-] Duplication of effort, loss of economies of sale
- [-] Loss of consistency/standardisation

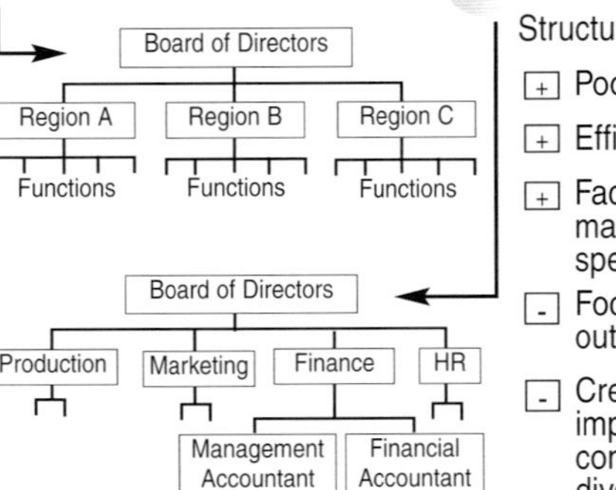

2 Functional structure

Structured according to **activity**

- [+] Pooling of specialist expertise
- [+] Efficient use of shared resources
- [+] Facilitates recruitment, management and development of specialist staff
- [-] Focuses on input/process, not outputs
- [-] Creates 'vertical' barriers: impedes workflow, coordination, communication, growth, diversification

3 Matrix structure

is a form of organisation which 'crosses' functional and divisional structures, forming multi-functional units (or teams), under the control of a product or project manager. Team members also report to their line manager on day-to-day operations.

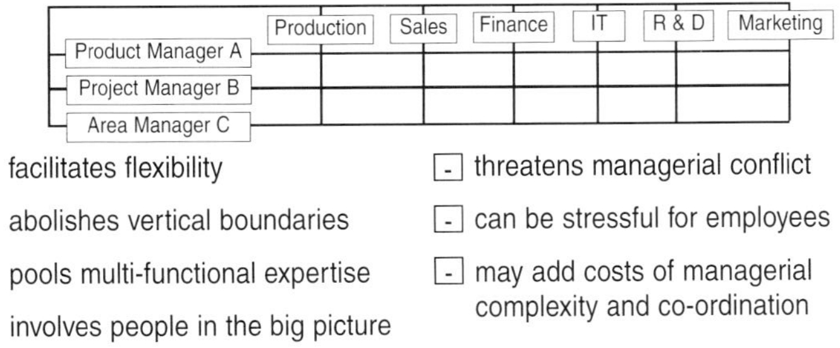

+ facilitates flexibility
+ abolishes vertical boundaries
+ pools multi-functional expertise
+ involves people in the big picture

- threatens managerial conflict
- can be stressful for employees
- may add costs of managerial complexity and co-ordination

Centralisation

refers to the concentration of authority in one place:

- geographically
- in the hierarchy of authority

Arguments pro centralisation

- Decisions easier to control and coordinate
- Senior managers have access to the 'big picture'
- Senior managers can balance demands of different functions
- Decisions may benefit from senior managers' experience/contacts
- May reduce overheads (fewer managerial salaries)
- Crisis decisions can be taken speedily (no reference)
- Policy decisions can be standardised organisation wide

Decentralisation

refers to the delegation or devolution of authority:

- to local business units
- to lower levels of the hierarchy

Arguments pro decentralisation

- Avoids overburdening senior managers with detail
- Improves motivation of subordinates given responsibility
- Decision makers are more aware of local/front-line issues
- Greater speed of decision-making (less reference upwards)
- Facilitates development/succession of junior managers
- More distinct areas of accountability for controls
- Supported by communications technology
- More flexible in the face of customer demands

TALL

MD
Divisional directors
Department managers
Section managers
Assistant managers
Supervisors/team leaders
Workers

FLAT

MD
Managers
Supervisors
Workers

Tall organisation

- [+] Narrow control spans → managerial control
- [+] Defined career ladder → employee loyalty
- [+] Specialisation → technical excellence
- [-] Close control fosters rigidity, blocks initiative
- [-] Increased administration and overhead costs
- [-] Lengthens communication and decision-making
- [-] Strategic apex distanced from the customer

Flat organisation

- [+] Strategic apex close to operating core
- [+] Strategic apex close to the customer
- [+] Savings on managerial costs
- [+] More opportunity for delegation/empowerment
- [-] Loss of managerial control
- [-] Loss of middle management interface
- [-] If delayered, loss of middle management knowledge

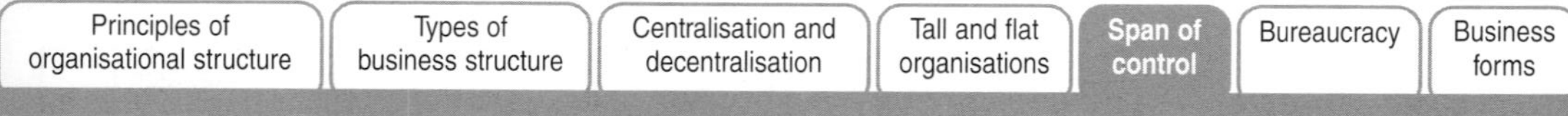

Span of control refers to the number of subordinates reporting to one manager

Influences on manager's span of control

- Manager's capability
- Nature of manager's work: higher degree of non-supervisory work = narrower span of control greater degree of delegation
- Geographical dispersion of staff
- Homogeneity of subordinates' tasks
- Degree of group cohesion required
- Nature of problems
- Degree of interaction between subordinates
- Support received from senior managers/technology

Managers' work

Solitary + External dealings + Internal interaction + Supervisory work

← Non-supervisory work

Ideal span of control (Urwich):

- Tight control from top to bottom
- Restrict span of control to 3-6 direct subordinates per manager
- Too wide → lack of time for planning
- Too narrow → lack of delegation = demotivating

Bureaucracy

is a *'continuous organisation* of *official functions* bound by *rules.'* (Max Weber)

Very stable, predictable

Efficient, safe
Technical competence

Impersonal, rational, fair
Hierarchical, specialised

Characteristics of bureaucracy

- Hierarchy of roles
- Specialisation/need for training
- Professional nature of employment
- Impersonal nature
- Rationality
- Uniformity in performance of tasks
- Technical competence
- Stability

Problems with bureaucracy

- Slow communication and decision-making
- Conformity (while 'safe') can inhibit growth, development
- Rigidity of rules leads to inability to change, adapt
- Restricted communication inhibits innovation
- Lack of feedback leads to inability to learn from mistakes

(Burns & Stalker) *'Mechanistic organisation'*

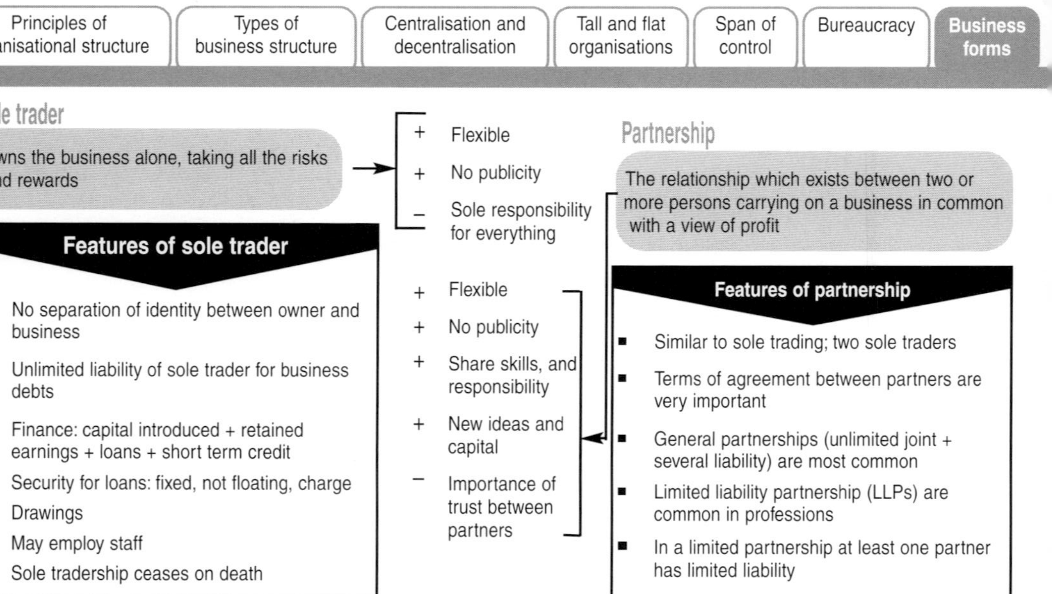
Principles of organisational structure
Types of business structure
Centralisation and decentralisation
Tall and flat organisations
Span of control
Bureaucracy
Business forms
Sole trader
Owns the business alone, taking all the risks and rewards
+ Flexible
+ No publicity
– Sole responsibility for everything
Features of sole trader
■ No separation of identity between owner and business
■ Unlimited liability of sole trader for business debts
■ Finance: capital introduced + retained earnings + loans + short term credit
■ Security for loans: fixed, not floating, charge
■ Drawings
■ May employ staff
■ Sole tradership ceases on death
Partnership
The relationship which exists between two or more persons carrying on a business in common with a view of profit
+ Flexible
+ No publicity
+ Share skills, and responsibility
+ New ideas and capital
– Importance of trust between partners
Features of partnership
■ Similar to sole trading; two sole traders
■ Terms of agreement between partners are very important
■ General partnerships (unlimited joint + several liability) are most common
■ Limited liability partnership (LLPs) are common in professions
■ In a limited partnership at least one partner has limited liability

Company

Features of a limited company

+	Company is legally distinct from its owners (members)
+	Members' liability for company's debts is limited to the amount unpaid, if any, on their shares
-	Separation of ownership (members) and control (directors)
-	Shareholders take dividends declared by directors
+	Shares are a form of property that can be transferred easily
+	Perpetual succession on members' death
+	Can give floating as well as fixed charges
-	Shareholders do not own assets; company does
-	Publicity (accounts and returns)
-	Regulation and expense

Alliances

Joint ventures are arrangements between businesses to pool their interests on a project. The mechanism is usually a subsidiary company.

Strategic alliances tend to be longer term and aim to complement technology, geography, markets and so on.

Advantages of alliances

- Coverage of a larger number of markets
- Reduced risk of government intervention
- Closer control over operations
- Local knowledge
- Spreading of risk and costs
- Learning from partners

However, there can be major conflicts of interest, and disagreements over:

- Profit sharing
- Investment levels
- Management
- Marketing strategy

Other arrangements include co-operative methods such as:

1. Licensing – the licenser provides rights, advice and know how in return for a royalty
2. Franchising – the franchiser provides expertise and brand, the franchisee provides capital
3. Sub-contracting – enhanced access to resources, reduce overheads
4. Agents – used as a distribution network

4: Introduction to business strategy

Topic List

- What is strategy?
- Strategic planning process
- External analysis
- Internal analysis
- Corporate appraisal
- Mission, goals and objectives
- Gap analysis
- Strategic options and choice

This substantial chapter covers the key elements of the strategic planning process, including many models which are highly examinable.

Planning

The establishment of objectives, and those policies, strategies, tactics and actions required to achieve them

is the basis for:

Managing business strategy

Strategy: course of action to achieve a specific objective

Strategic plan: statement of long term goals, and those policies which will ensure their achievement

Strategic management: management of the elements involved in planning and controlling a business strategy: taking decisions about the business's scope and long-term future, and allocating resources

Benefits of formal strategic management

- Coherent response to change
- Best use of limited resources
- Fit business to environment
- Avoid short-termism
- Ensure goal congruence

Drawbacks of formal strategic management

- Expense of time + money
- Slow and undynamic process
- Discourages opportunism and innovation
- Less relevant in a crisis
- May seem irrelevant to lower management levels (lack of goal congruence)
- Managers do not know everything
- Activities are not rational and logical
- Long-term plans are undermined by short-term events

The emergent approach:

Letting strategy 'emerge' is an alternative approach emphasising:

- Adaptability
- Evolution
- Creativity
- Pragmatism

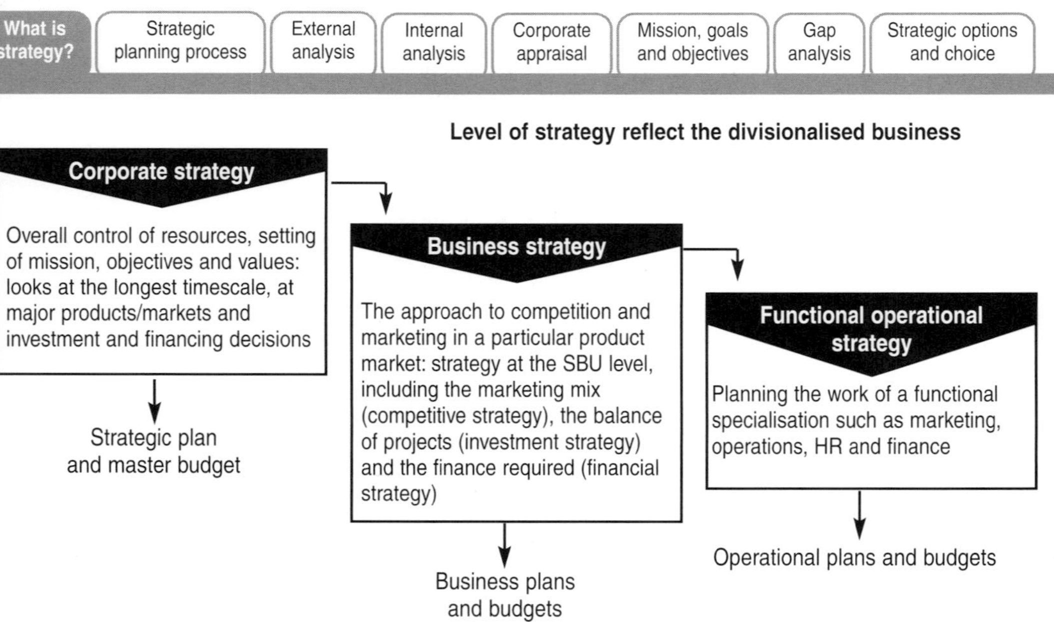
Level of strategy reflect the divisionalised business
Corporate strategy
Overall control of resources, setting of mission, objectives and values: looks at the longest timescale, at major products/markets and investment and financing decisions
Strategic plan and master budget
Business strategy
The approach to competition and marketing in a particular product market: strategy at the SBU level, including the marketing mix (competitive strategy), the balance of projects (investment strategy) and the finance required (financial strategy)
Business plans and budgets
Functional operational strategy
Planning the work of a functional specialisation such as marketing, operations, HR and finance
Operational plans and budgets

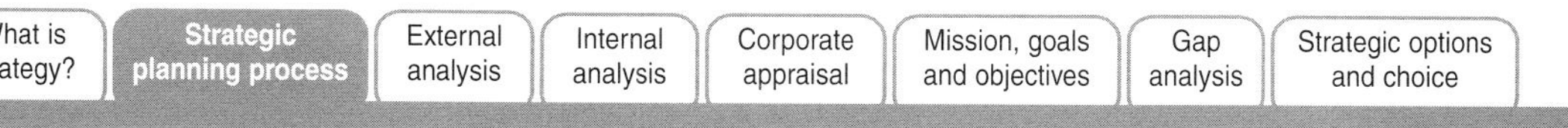

Positioning-based view

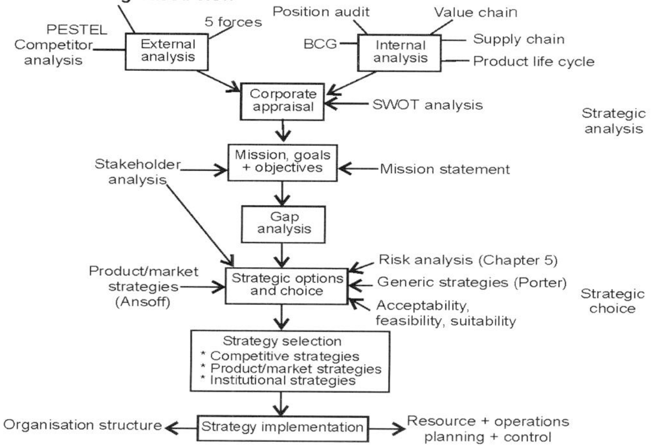

PESTEL
Competitor analysis
5 forces
External analysis
Position audit
BCG
Value chain
Supply chain
Product life cycle
Internal analysis
Corporate appraisal
SWOT analysis
Strategic analysis
Stakeholder analysis
Mission, goals + objectives
Mission statement
Gap analysis
Product/market strategies (Ansoff)
Strategic options and choice
Risk analysis (Chapter 5)
Generic strategies (Porter)
Acceptability, feasibility, suitability
Strategic choice
Strategy selection
* Competitive strategies
* Product/market strategies
* Institutional strategies
Organisation structure
Strategy implementation
Resource + operations planning + control

The business must analyse its external general and task environment.

General environment

Includes political, legal, economic, social, ecological and technological factors (PESTEL)

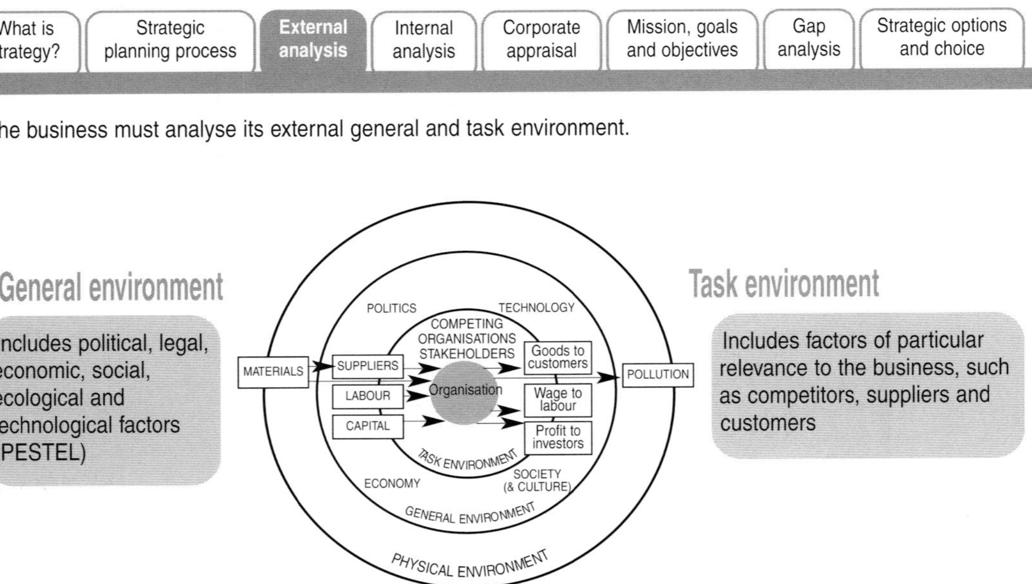

Task environment

Includes factors of particular relevance to the business, such as competitors, suppliers and customers

PESTEL analysis

Political factors

- Capacity expansion
- Demand
- Divestment/rationalisation
- Emerging industries
- Entry barriers
- Competition

Legal factors

- Legal framework: contract, tort, agency
- Criminal law
- Company law
- Employment
- Health & Safety
- Data and consumer protection
- Environment
- Tax law

Economic factors

- Local economic trends: working population and skills, cost of living
- Inflation
- Interest rates
- Tax levels
- Government spending
- Business cycle
- Productivity

Government policy

- Fiscal policy (taxes, borrowing, spending)
- Monetary policy (interest rates, exchange rates)
- Size and scope of the public sector
- Regulation

Social factors – demography

- Growth
- Age
- Geography
- Household structure
- Social structure
- Employment
- Wealth

Technological factors

- Rate of change
- Types of product/service
- Production, materials/equipment/processes
- Communication
- Delivery

Economic factors

- Resources
- Waste
- Regulation
- Disasters
- Demand
- Pressure groups

Five forces (Porter)

Forces that together determine the long term profit potential of an **industry**

Bargaining power of suppliers

Depends on:

- Number of suppliers
- Threats to suppliers industry
- Number of customers in the industry
- Scope for substitution
- Switching costs
- Selling skills

Suppliers seek **higher prices**

Threat of new entrants

This is limited by **barriers to entry**

- Scale economies
- Switching costs
- Patent rights
- Product differentiation
- Access to distribution
- Access to resources

Rivalry among current competitors

Depends on:

- Market growth
- Spare capacity
- Uncertainty
- Buyers ease of switching
- Exit barriers
- Cost structure

Threat from substitute products

A substitute is produced by a different industry but satisfies the same needs

Bargaining power of customers

Depends on:

- Volume bought
- Scope for substitution
- Switching costs
- Purchasing skills
- Importance of quality

Customers seek **lower prices**

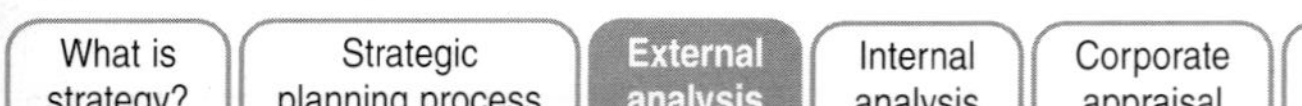

Competitor analysis

Types of competitor (Kotler)

- Brand: McDonald's v Burger King
- Industry: Amazon v Borders
- Generic: HMV v Books etc
- Form: matches v cigarette lighters

For each competitor, the business must analyse:

- Its strategy, including its structure and purpose
- Its assumptions about the industry
- Its current and potential situation
- Its capability
- Its response profile
  - Laid back?
  - Tiger?
  - Selective?
  - Stochastic?

Position audit

Examination of the business's current state in terms of resources and competencies

Some resources are easy to define, identify and measure (eg plant and machinery, finance). Others are more problematic, such as management skills, technical competence and culture.

Resource: Ms model

Materials – costs, security of supply
Men and women – skills, morale
Management – skills, capacity
Machinery – age, efficiency
Money – sources, gearing, cash flow
Make-up – brands, patents, culture, structure
Management information – ideas, innovation, systems
Markets – products, customers
Methods – processes, activities

- Resources are only of value if they are properly organised: **management** and **organisation** are vital resources.

Limiting factors

A factor which at any time or over a period may limit the activity of an entity, often one where there is a shortage or difficulty of supply

Resources should be used **efficiently**; this requires:

- **Effectiveness** – the measure of achievement
- **Economy** – containment of cost

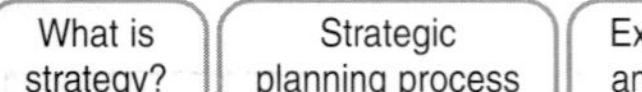

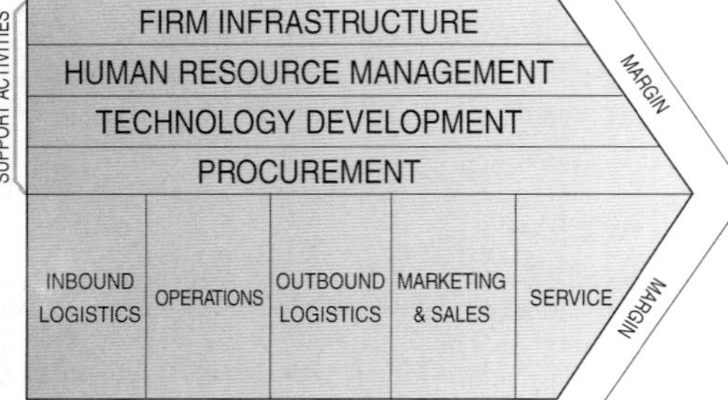

The **margin** is the excess the customer is prepared to **pay** over the **cost** to the firm of obtaining resource inputs and providing value activities. It represents the **value created** by the **value activities** themselves and by the **management of the linkages** between them. **Linkages** connect the activities in the value chain. The activities affect one another and therefore must be co-ordinated.

A firm's value chain is connected to what *Porter* calls a **value system.**

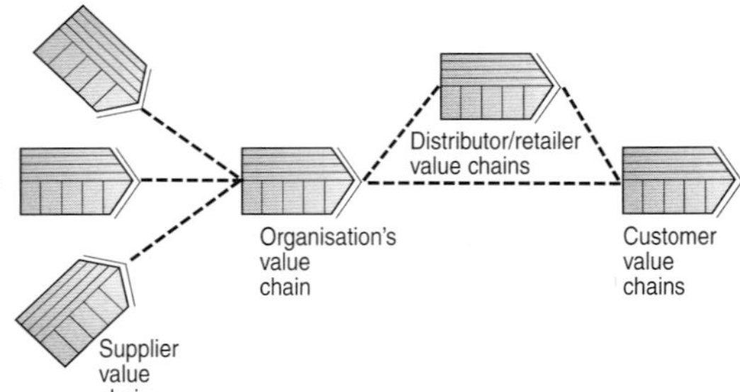

Using the value chain. A firm can secure competitive advantage in several ways.

- Invent new or better ways to do activities
- Combine activities in new or better ways
- Manage the linkages in its own value chain
- Manage the linkages in the value system

Supply chain

A **network between businesses**, rather than a **pipeline**, of close links and greater co-operation.

Supply chain management

Optimising the activities of businesses working together to produce goods and services.

Suppliers

This can be achieved via

- Reduction in number of suppliers partnering
- Reduction in number of customers
- Price and inventory co-ordination
- Linked computer systems
- Early supplier involvement in product development and design
- Logistics design
- Joint problem solving
- Supplier representative on site

Customers

Product life cycle

The company's offerings to the market are fundamental to its success. They must be kept under review so that there is a suitable mix. The **product life cycle** is an important concept but it must be applied with care. We can distinguish 3 aspects of 'product'.

Product class (or **generic product**)
A broad category

Product form
Type within the category

Brand
The specific product

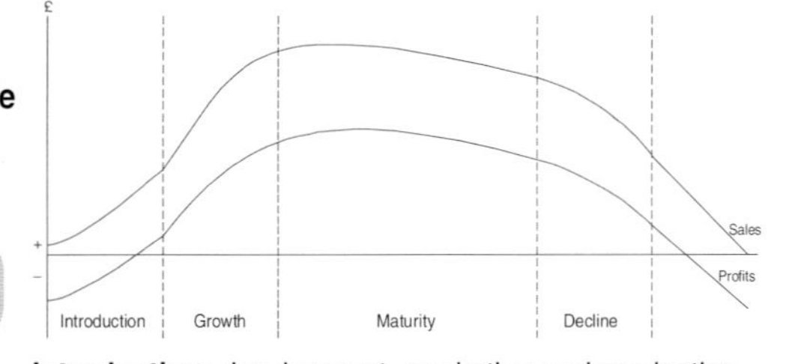

Introduction: development, marketing and production costs high; sales volume low; profits low

Growth: sales volumes accelerate, must costs fall, profits rise; competitors enter the market

Maturity: longest period; profits good, reminder promotion

Decline: many causes; sales fall, overcapacity in industry; some players leave market

BCG matrix is applicable to products, market segments and SBUs. There are four basic strategies:

Build
Invest for market share growth

Hold
Maintain current position

Harvest
Manage for profit in the short term

Divest
Release resources for use elsewhere

The BCG Matrix

Market growth			
	High	Star	Question mark
	Low	Cash cow	Dog
		High	Low

Market share relative to largest competitor

Stars – build
Cash cows – hold or harvest
Question marks – hold or harvest
Dogs – divest or hold

Corporate appraisal draws together the internal and external assessments in an analysis of strengths, weaknesses, opportunities and threats (SWOT analysis). A good strategy will utilise strengths to exploit opportunities while evading threats and minimising the effect of weaknesses.

SWOT analysis

A review of:

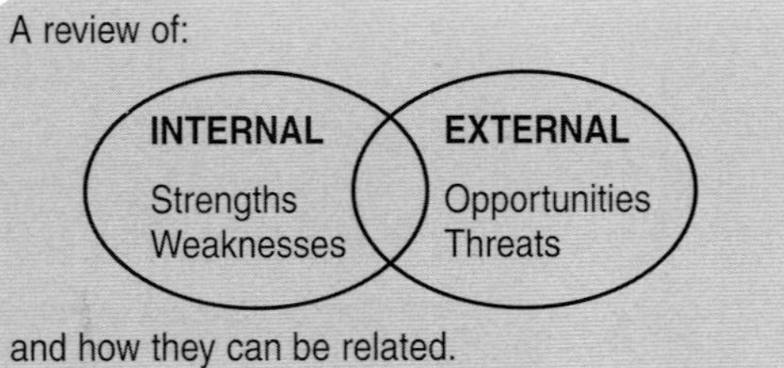

and how they can be related.

The results can be combined in the SWOT framework.

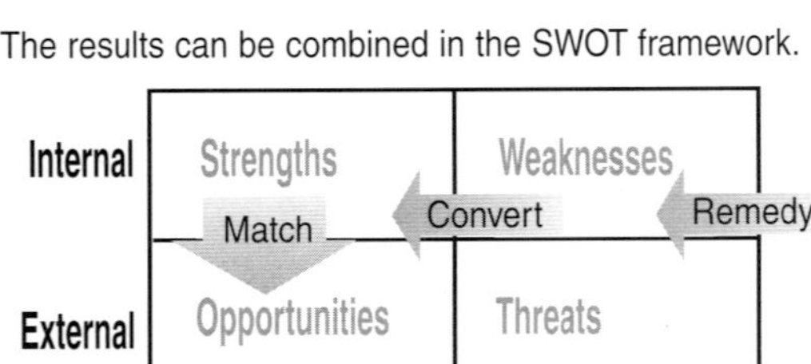

Stakeholder analysis (Mendelow)

Stakeholders' interests are likely to conflict. *Mendelow's* **stakeholder analysis** helps the business identify the key stakeholders and their sources of power when setting missions, goals and objectives.

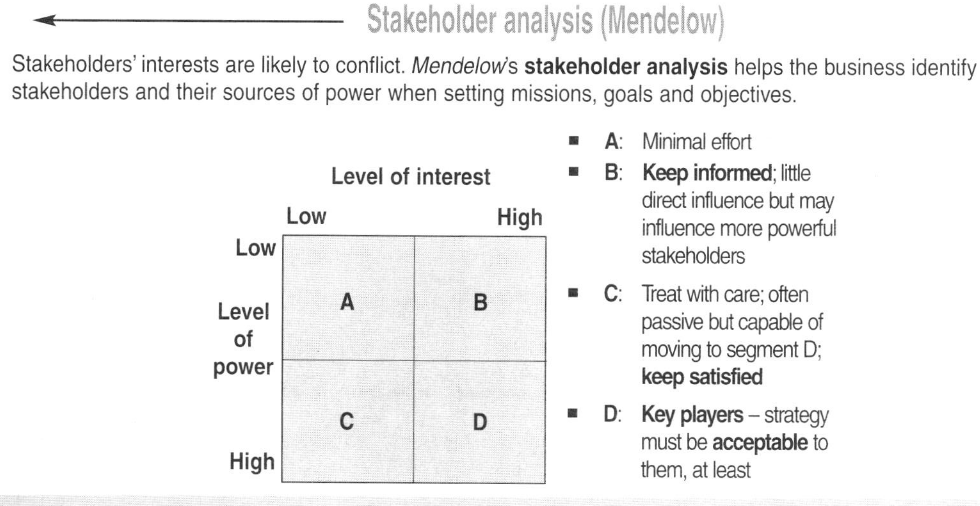

- A: Minimal effort
- B: **Keep informed**; little direct influence but may influence more powerful stakeholders
- C: Treat with care; often passive but capable of moving to segment D; **keep satisfied**
- D: **Key players** – strategy must be **acceptable** to them, at least

Hierarchy of objectives and strategies (top-down)

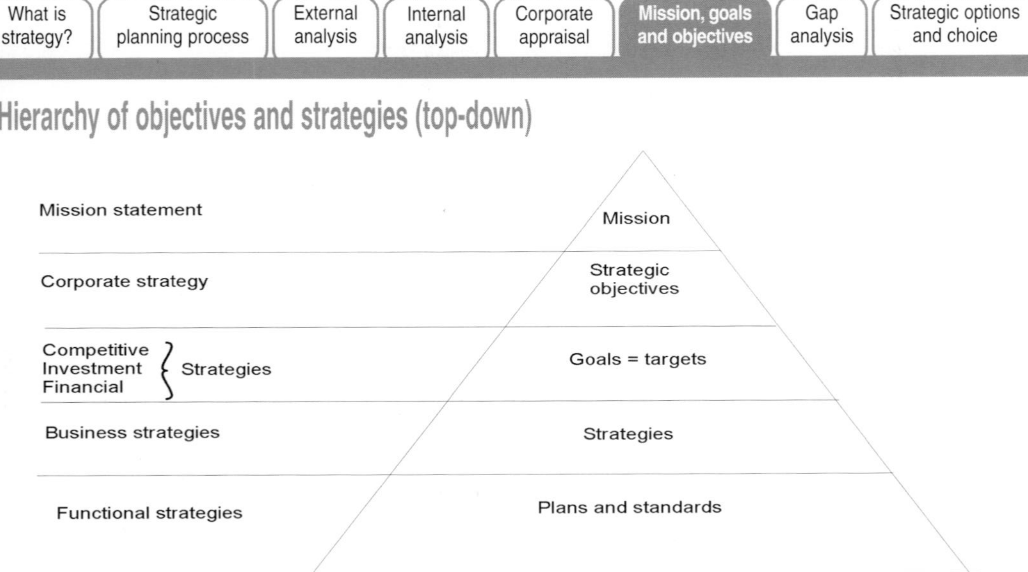

Mission statement

'The organisation's basic function in society' (*Mintzberg*)

Includes, typically:

- Purpose
- Basic strategy eg products
- Policies and standards of behaviour
- Values and culture
  - – business principles
  - – internal relationships
  - – behaviour

A formal **mission statement** may:

- Impress customers
- Motivate staff
- Guide manager's actions
- Guide strategic thinking

BUT it may also:

- Be ignored in practice
- Treated cynically as mere PR
- Merely rationalise what is done anyway
- Be the same as everyone else's

Strategic objectives and corporate strategy

The primary objective – maximising shareholder wealth – plus other major objectives arising from stakeholder analysis, formulated as **corporate strategy**

Strategic objectives are broken down into goals, targets, plans and standards.

Remember the corporate strategy is broken down into **business strategies** for each SBU

↓ Competitive strategy

↓ Investment strategy

↓ Financial strategy

Gap analysis

A comparison of a business's desired future profit and the expected profits of projects currently planned or underway.

The profit gap is the difference between the target profits and the profits on the forecast.

(a) First of all the business can estimate the effects on the gap of any projects or strategies in the pipeline. Some of the gap might be filled by a new project.

(b) Then, if a gap remains, new strategies have to be considered to close the gap.

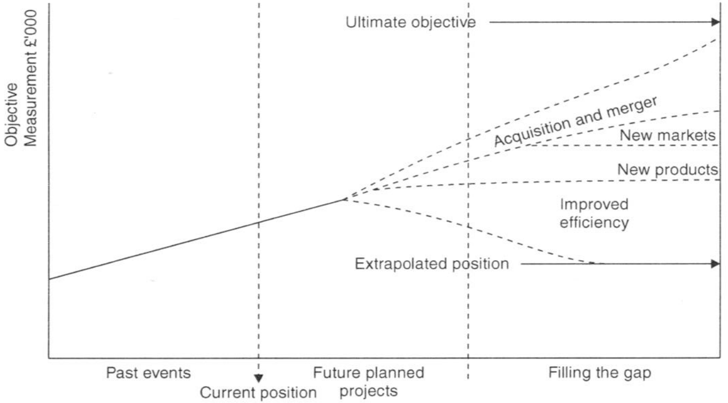

Generic strategies and the five competitive forces (Porter)

Generic strategies

- Cost leadership - producing at lowest cost in the industry
- Differentiation providing a unique product/service
- Focus/niche - restricting activities to a segment using either a cost leadership or a differentiation-focus

Competitive force	*Cost leadership*	*Differentiation*
New entrants	+ Economies of scale raise entry barriers	+ Brand loyalty and perceived uniqueness are entry barriers
Substitutes	+ Firm is not so vulnerable as its less cost-effective competitors to the threat of substitutes	+ Customer loyalty is a weapon against substitutes
Customers	+ Customers cannot drive down prices further than the next most efficient competitor	+ Customers have no comparable alternative + Brand loyalty should lower price sensitivity – Customers may no longer need the differentiating factor – Sooner or later, customers become price sensitive
Suppliers	+ Flexibility to deal with cost increases – Higher margins can offset vulnerability to supplier price rises	Increase in input costs can reduce price advantages
Industry rivalry	+ Firms remains profitable when rivals go under through excessive price competition – Technological change will require capital investment, or make production cheaper for competitors – Competitors learn via imitation – Cost concerns ignore product design or marketing issues	+ Unique features reduce direct competition – Imitation narrows differentiation

Product/market strategies (Ansoff)

Ansoff described the four possible growth vectors in the four cells in the diagram below. Numbers in circles show relative riskiness.

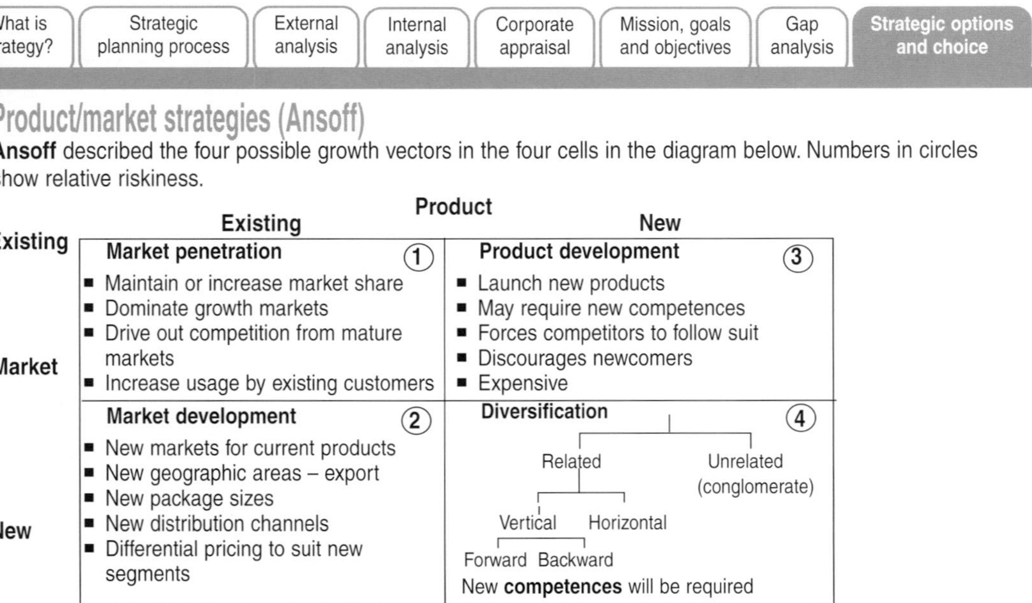

Market \ Product	Existing	New
Existing	**Market penetration** ① ■ Maintain or increase market share ■ Dominate growth markets ■ Drive out competition from mature markets ■ Increase usage by existing customers	**Product development** ③ ■ Launch new products ■ May require new competences ■ Forces competitors to follow suit ■ Discourages newcomers ■ Expensive
New	**Market development** ② ■ New markets for current products ■ New geographic areas – export ■ New package sizes ■ New distribution channels ■ Differential pricing to suit new segments	**Diversification** ④ Related: Vertical (Forward, Backward), Horizontal Unrelated (conglomerate) New **competences** will be required

Evaluating alternative strategies (Johnson and Scholes)

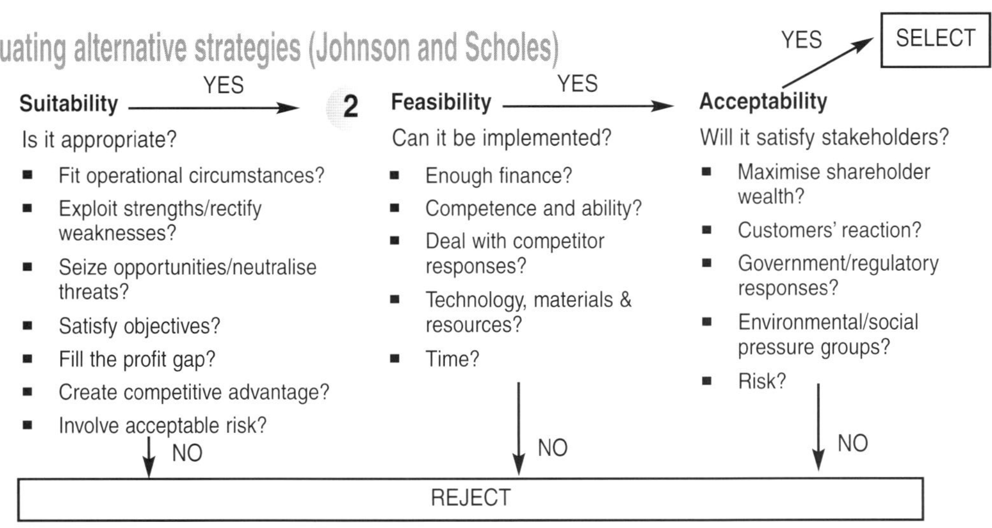

Notes

5: Introduction to risk management

Topic List

- What is risk?
- Risk appetite
- Risk classifications
- Managing risk
- Crisis management

Risk analysis is part of the strategic planning process, and risk is also an important element in working capital management and in corporate governance.

In this chapter we introduce what is meant by the term 'risk', and how it can be managed.

Risk

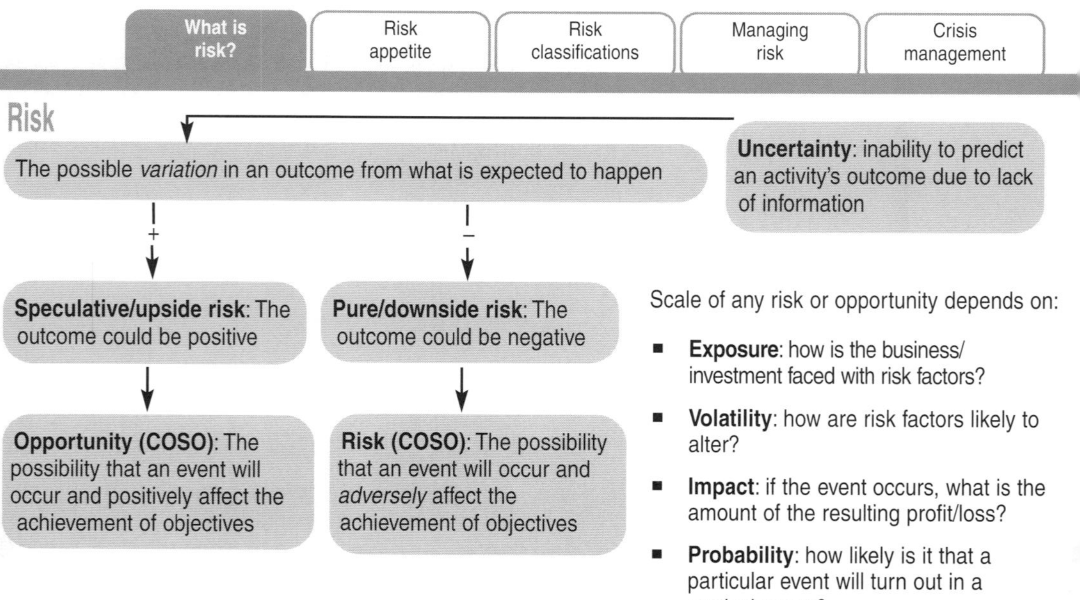

Scale of any risk or opportunity depends on:

- **Exposure**: how is the business/investment faced with risk factors?
- **Volatility**: how are risk factors likely to alter?
- **Impact**: if the event occurs, what is the amount of the resulting profit/loss?
- **Probability**: how likely is it that a particular event will turn out in a particular way?

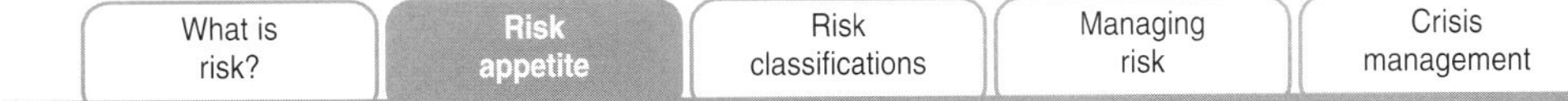

Management set objectives

Identify/assess risks to achievement of objectives

Risk appetite is the extent to which the business is prepared to take on risks in order to achieve objectives

Risk averse → Select least risky investment

Risk neutral → Select investment with highest **expected returns**

Risk seeking → Select highest risk investment

Expected return: weighted average of possible returns x probability of each occurring

Risk

Business risk

- *Strategy risk*: choosing the wrong corporate, business or functional strategy
- *Enterprise risk*: a project fails because it should not have been taken on
- *Product risk*: product/services will not appeal to customers
- *Economic risk*: economic conditions change unexpectedly
- *Technology risk*: change in production/delivery technology
- *Property risk*: loss of or damage to property

Non-business risk

Financial risk

- Liquidity
- Gearing
- Default
- Credit
- Foreign exchange
- Interest rate
- Market

Operational risk

- Process
- People
- Systems
- Legal
- Event

FINANCIAL RISK

Gearing risk

- High debt/equity ratio increasing volatility + risk of insolvency

Default risk

- Receivables may not pay what they owe at all/on time

Liquidity risk

- Unexpected shortage of cash

Credit risk

- Company's credit rating is downgraded, restricting access to credit and/or making it more expensive

Market risk

- Share prices move adversely

Interest rate risk

- Changes in interest rates cause unexpected losses

Foreign exchange risk

- Changes in exchange rate cause unexpected losses

OPERATIONAL RISK

Process risk

- Organisation's processes may be ineffective/inefficient

People risk

- Risks from staff constraints, incompetence, dishonesty

Disaster risk

- Risk of loss due to single, unlikely event, which may have serious consequences.

Systems risk

- Risks arising from information and communications systems

Event risk

- Risk of loss due to single event

Regulatory risk

- New regulations affect operations

Legal risk

- Risk of loss from contract that cannot legally be enforced

Reputation risk

- Business activities damage its reputation in stakeholders' eyes

Systematic risk

- Failure in business's systems or supply chain

Disaster risk = risk of loss due to single, unlikely event, which may have serious consequences.

Fire

- Site preparation eg fire proof materials
- Detection eg smoke detectors
- Extinguishers eg sprinklers

Water

- Waterproof ceilings
- Adequate drainage

Other measures

- Physical access controls
- Good office layout
- Protected power supplies
- Separate generator

Disaster recovery plan

- **Responsibilities** including overall manager and subordinates
- **Priorities** – establish most important tasks needing computer time
- **Backup/standby** – with other company/manual processing
- **Communication** – tell staff details/implications/actions
- **Public relations** – managing external concerns
- **Risk assessment** – risk of recurrence of problem/occurrence elsewhere in organisation

Risk management

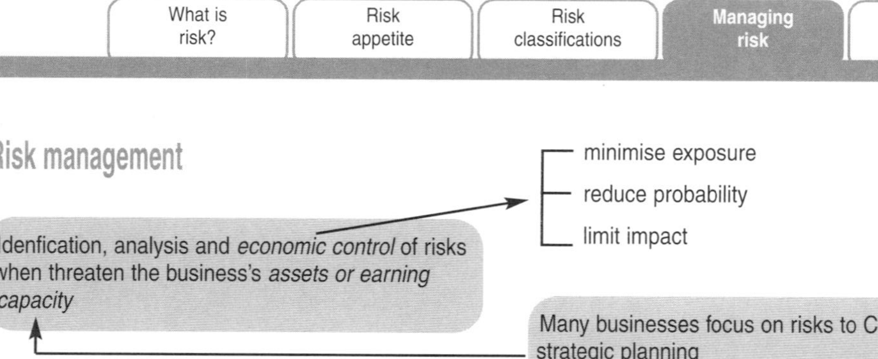

A business may be required to manage risks formally by:

- The law (car insurance)
- Regulatory bodies (ICAEW require PII; FRC Combined Code requires risk-based management approach to corporate governance)
- Contract (mortgages require buildings insurance)

Risk management process

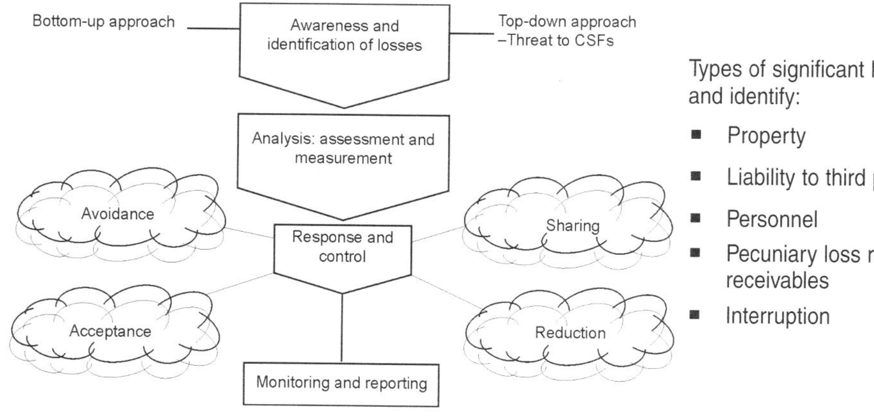

Types of significant loss to be aware of and identify:

- Property
- Liability to third parties
- Personnel
- Pecuniary loss regarding receivables
- Interruption

Risk assessment

Consider the nature of each risk, its implications and its potential seriousness

Risk measurement

Identify the probability of the risk occurring and quantify the resultant impact

Probability x Impact = **Expected value** of **gross risk** (uncontrolled)

Risk response & control

- **Risk avoidance** – Not investing in high risk/high cost operations
- **Risk reduction** – Contingency planning, physical measures (alarms, fire precautions) awareness and commitment
- **Risk acceptance/retention** – Bear full cost if risk materialises; valid if risks insignificant or avoidance costs too great
- **Risk transfer/sharing** – to suppliers, customers, insurers, state; with insurers/joint venture partners

Risk monitoring & reporting

Monitoring should be ongoing and continuous; action should be taken promptly as a result (= control):

- Corrective action on risk
- Review of identification and response processes

Risk management issues must be reported to the appropriate persons in management hierarchy

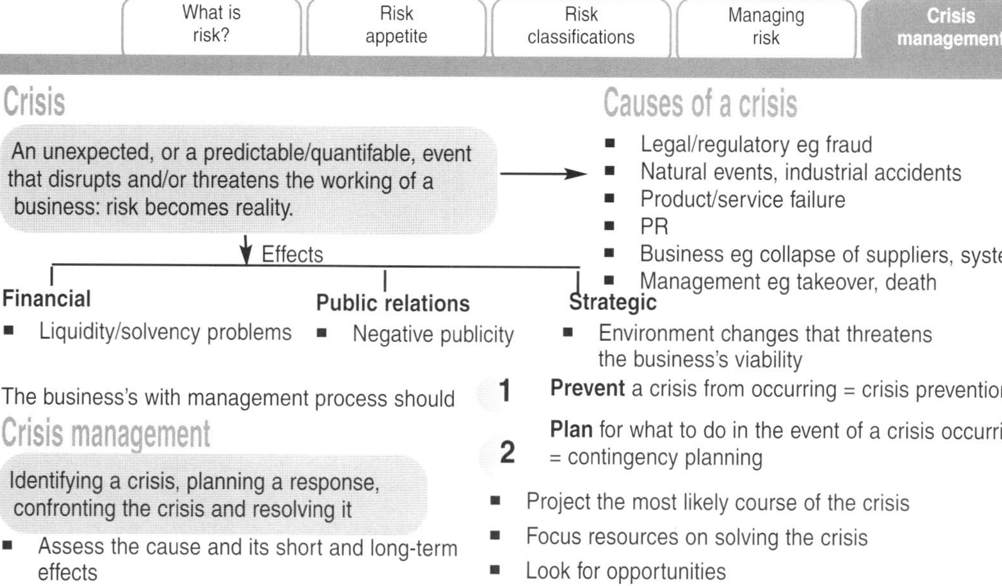

Crisis

An unexpected, or a predictable/quantifable, event that disrupts and/or threatens the working of a business: risk becomes reality.

Effects

Financial

- Liquidity/solvency problems

Public relations

- Negative publicity

Strategic

- Environment changes that threatens the business's viability

Causes of a crisis

- Legal/regulatory eg fraud
- Natural events, industrial accidents
- Product/service failure
- PR
- Business eg collapse of suppliers, systems
- Management eg takeover, death

The business's with management process should

1 **Prevent** a crisis from occurring = crisis prevention

2 **Plan** for what to do in the event of a crisis occurring = contingency planning

Crisis management

Identifying a crisis, planning a response, confronting the crisis and resolving it

- Assess the cause and its short and long-term effects
- Project the most likely course of the crisis
- Focus resources on solving the crisis
- Look for opportunities

Notes

6: Introduction to financial information

Topic List

- Financial information
- Information systems
- Information security
- Uses of financial information
- Financial statements

The production of financial information lies at the heart of accountancy. In this chapter we look at types of financial information and their uses, at information systems and security, and at the uses of financial statements.

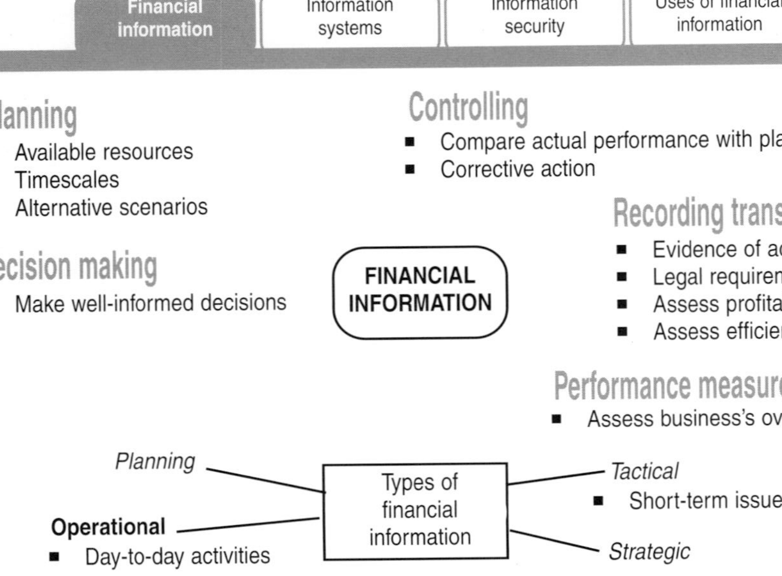

FINANCIAL INFORMATION
Planning
Available resources
Timescales
Alternative scenarios
Decision making
Make well-informed decisions
Controlling
Compare actual performance with plan
Corrective action
Recording transactions
Evidence of activity
Legal requirement
Assess profitability
Assess efficiency
Performance measurement
Assess business's overall performance
Types of financial information
Planning
Operational
Day-to-day activities
Tactical
Short-term issues + opportunities
Strategic
Long-term decisions

Qualities of good financial information: ACCURATE

Accurate: adding-up, rounding, error-free, properly categorised, state assumptions, identify uncertainty

Complete: include everything needed, such as external data, comparatives

Cost-beneficial: benefits of having information > costs of obtaining it; efficient collection and analysis

User-targeted: needs of user should be met eg detailed or summarised?

Relevant: unnecessary information should be omitted

Authoritative: reliable sources

Timely: should be available when it is needed

Easy to use: clear presentation; no longer than necessary; sent in appropriate form, medium and channel

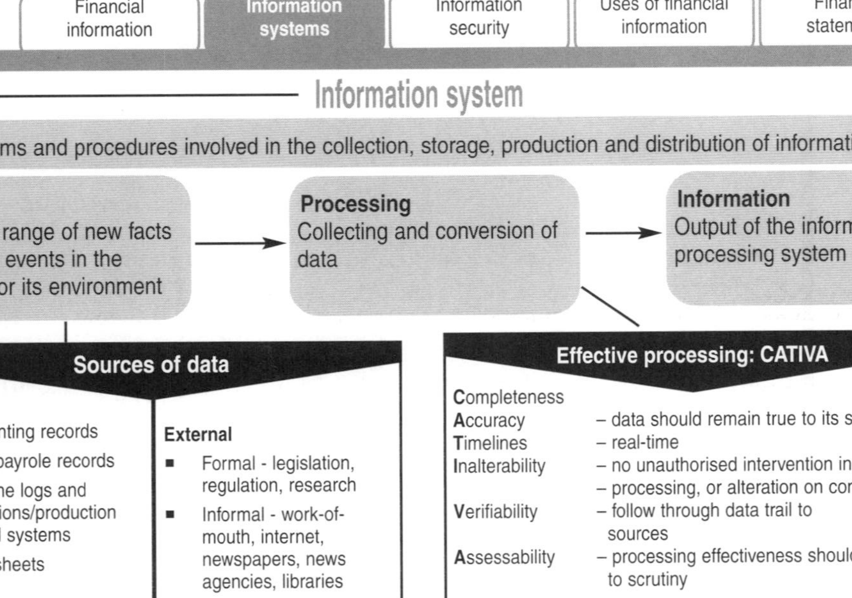
Financial information
Information systems
Information security
Uses of financial information
Financial statements
Information system
All systems and procedures involved in the collection, storage, production and distribution of information
Data
Complete range of new facts relating to events in the business or its environment
Processing
Collecting and conversion of data
Information
Output of the information processing system
Sources of data
Internal
Accounting records
HR + payrole records
Machine logs and operations/production control systems
Time sheets
Staff
External
Formal - legislation, regulation, research
Informal - work-of-mouth, internet, newspapers, news agencies, libraries
Effective processing: CATIVA
Completeness
Accuracy – data should remain true to its sources
Timelines – real-time
Inalterability – no unauthorised intervention in
– processing, or alteration on completion
Verifiability – follow through data trail to sources
Assessability – processing effectiveness should be open to scrutiny

Transaction processing system (TPS)

Performs, records and processes routine transactions

Uses of TPS

- Sales/marketing: eg sales management, promotion pricing
- Production: eg scheduling, procurement, engineering
- Finance: eg nominal ledger, invoicing, budgeting
- HR: eg payroll, personnel records, training

Management information system (MIS)

Converts internal data into information for managers to plan, control, organise and lead the business

Uses of MIS

- Support structured decisions
- Reports on existing, internal operations

Expert system

Database of specialised data/information plus rules on what to do in a given set of circumstances, provided problem is reasonably well-defined

Uses of expert system

- Legal/tax advice
- Forecasting
- Surveillance
- Diagnostic systems
- Project management
- Education and training

Information security

The system, and the information held on it, must be protected from unauthorised modification, theft, unavailability, and/or destruction. The aim is to ensure the availability of efficient service at all times.

Aspects of security

- Prevention
- Detection
- Deterrence
- Recovery procedures
- Correction procedures
- Threat avoidance

Qualities of a secure information system: ACIANA

Availability

Confidentiality

Integrity – information is true to its data source

Authenticity – sources are *bone fide*

Non-repudiation – users accept information as being from a secure system

Authorisation – changes can only be made by persons who are accountable

Physical access controls

Physical access controls are designed to prevent intruders accessing computer equipment and storage

- Personnel – receptionists and security guards
- Door locks
- Keypad access system
- Card entry system
- Intruder alarms
- Personnel identification systems

Theft precautions

- Log off computer equipment/software
- Smaller items locked away
- Secure disk store
- Check licensed

Passwords

Logical access system enabling

- Identification of user
- Authentication of user identity
- Checks on user authority
- Restrictions of tasks/access to parts of system

Problems with passwords

- Some can be guessed easily
- Standard passwords not removed
- Users tell unauthorised persons
- Passwords left lying around

Built-in controls

Integrity controls

- Data verification and validation
- Input checks
  - Check digits
  - Hash tables
  - Control totals
  - Range checks
  - Limit checks
- Processing (batch) controls
- Output controls (eg audit trail)
- Back-up routines + off-site storage
- Disaster recovery plans

Security controls

- Physical security
- Logical access controls (eg passwords)
- Personnel selection
- Segregation of duties

Controls help prevent:

- Human error
- Technical error
- Fraud
- Espionage
- Malicious damage

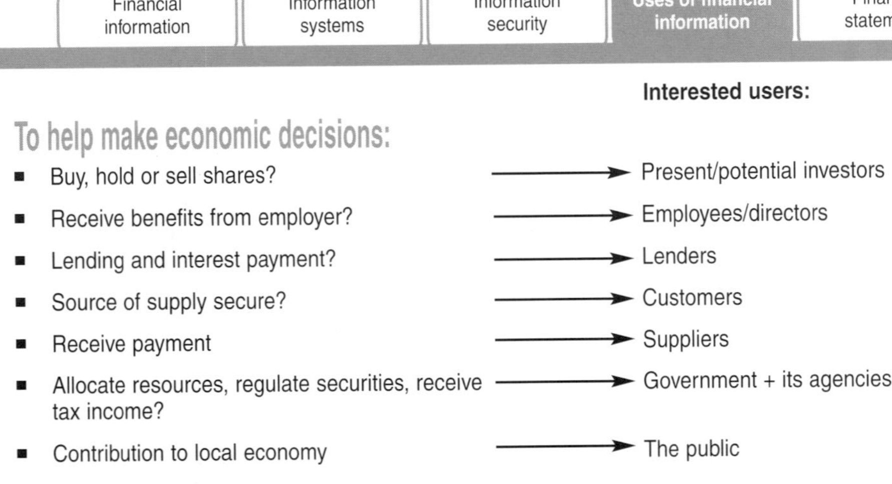
Interested users:
1 To help make economic decisions:
Buy, hold or sell shares? → Present/potential investors
Receive benefits from employer? → Employees/directors
Lending and interest payment? → Lenders
Source of supply secure? → Customers
Receive payment → Suppliers
Allocate resources, regulate securities, receive tax income? → Government + its agencies
Contribution to local economy → The public
2 To help make managers accountable for their stewardship of business's resources → All

To make *economic decisions* users need to evaluate the *ability* of the business to generate cash, and the *timing* and *certainty* of cash flows. Therefore they need information contained in **financial statements**.

4A Financial position = balance sheet

Relevant factors	Information needed to predict
■ Economic resources controlled	■ Ability to generate cash in future
■ Financial structure	■ Borrowing, distribution of profit, new equity
■ Liquidity	■ Availability of positive net cash in near future
■ Solvency	■ Availability of positive net cash in longer term
■ Adaptability	■ Capacity to adapt to environment changes

4B Financial performance = income statement

Information on variability in profitability helps user to predict:

- Changes in economic resources
- Capacity to generate cash from existing resources
- How well it might use new resources

4C Changes in financial position = cash flow statement

Information on past cash flows helps user to assess:

- How able it is at generating cash
- How well it uses generated cash

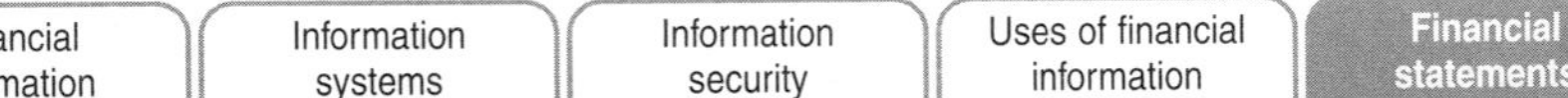

Qualitative characteristics

The attributes that make information in financial statements useful

Understandability
(for a reasonably knowledgeable and diligent user)

Relevance
to evaluation of past, present and future events.

Affected by:

- **nature** of certain items
- **materiality** of certain items

Reliability

- Free from material error
- Neutral (free from bias)
- Faithful presentation
- Substance over form
- Completeness
- Prudence

Comparability

- Throughout business
- Over time
- With other businesses

Constraints

- Timeliness – delay impairs relevance
  – haste impairs reliability
- Balance of benefit v cost

Limitations in meeting users' needs

1 *Conventionalised representation*

- highly standardised
- highly aggregated

2 *Backward-looking*

- historical focus, not on future

3 *Omission of non-financial information*

- Narrative descriptions
- Risks and opportunities
- Analysis of performance and prospects
- Governance

usually covered in Chairman's Statement and Directors' Report

Effects of poor financial information

- Fails to meet users' needs
- Is not understandable, relevant, reliable or comparable

so

- **integrity of financial markets** is undermined
- **public interest** is not served

7: The business's finance function

Topic List

- The finance function
- Management accounting
- Financial control processes

The business's finance function, like its marketing, operations and HR functions, has certain tasks to be managed. In this chapter we concentrate on the task of management accounting.

Tasks of finance function

1. *Recording financial transactions* and *controlling resources*
2. *Management accounting for internal users*
   - Internal reporting for management and control
   - Cost accounting
   - Forecasting and budgets
   - Assist with decision making
   - Measuring performance
   - Analysing investment decisions
   - Pricing
3. *Treasury management*
   - Preparing cash budgets
   - Managing surpluses/deficits of cash, and investment
   - Managing inventory, receivables and payables to optimise cash flow
   - Analysing financing decisions
   - Managing foreign exchange
   - Managing financial risk
   - Raising long-term debt/equity finance
4. *Financial reporting to external users*
   - Financial statements
   - Tax
   - Regulatory

Purpose of finance function

To support pursuit of business objective by

- Providing information for *planning/control*, *decision making*, *performance measurement*
- Ensuring there is sufficient *liquidity and solvency*

Providing information to the business's managers, to assist decision-making, planning and control

1 Cost accounting

- Attaching cost information to *cost units* (each unit of output) eg to assist pricing
- Establishing *budgets*, *standards* and *actual costs* of operations/processes/activities/products
- Analysing *variances* and *profitability*
- *Valuing* assets eg inventory
- *Classifying costs*

Nature

- Materials
- Labour
- Expense

Function

- Cost of sales
- Administrative
- Distribution costs

Direct/indirect

Fixed/variable/semi-variable

Controllable/uncontrollable

2 Establishing costs for decision-making

Relevant costs

- Future costs
- Avoidable costs
- Differential/marginal costs
- Opportunity costs

Irrelevant costs

- Sunk costs
- Unavoidable costs

3 Making resource decisions in short/medium term: cost-volume-profit (CVP) analysis

Aim: maximise revenue + minimise variable cost = maximise contribution to fixed costs

Per unit:	£		*Business as whole:*	£
Selling price	X			
Variable cost	(X)	= marginal cost	= Total contribution	X
Contribution per unit	X	x volume of sales	Fixed costs	(X)
			Net profit	X

Breakeven analysis: determines the levels of production/sales at which neither profit nor loss occurs (Contribution = fixed costs) to decide whether to proceed with new product

Contribution analysis: determines the effects of changes in sales prices, variable costs or fixed costs

Limiting factor analysis: determines the contribution made per unit of a factor in short supply (labour or materials) to decide what to produce

4 Making investment decisions for the long-term

To make a long-term investment the business needs:

- Sufficient long-term funds: *capital budgeting*

	£
+ Capital inflows (retained earnings, share issues, loans, sales of non-current asset)	X
– Capital outflows (purchase of non-current assets, repay loans)	(X)
New capital required	X

- To be sure investment is worthwhile: *investment appraisal*
  - Payback method – how soon is initial investment repaid?
  - Discounted cash flow – are future cash flows positive once the effects of time and risk are taken into account (net present value or NPV)? What will the investment earn (internal rate of return or IRR)?

To meet objective of maximising shareholder wealth, any investment should aim to *maximise the present value of future cash flows.*

5 Pricing

Influences on pricing policy

- Costs: price above total cost, our cost or at least at marginal cost
- Competitor prices
- Customer expectations
- Corporate objectives - maximise profits, achieve target return, revenue or market share?

Factors affecting demand

In business's control

- Price of item
- Marketing research
- Partner research & development
- Advertising
- Sales promotion
- Sales force
- Distribution
- After-sales service
- Customer credit

Outside business's control

- Price of substitutes
- Price of complements
- Incomes
- Taste and fashion

See Chapter 14

6 Budgeting

A **budget** is a plan expressed in monetary terms

Purposes of budgets

- To compel planning
- To co-ordinate activities
- To communicate plans
- To set targets and allocate responsibility
- To motivate employees/management
- To evaluate performance
- To guide managers on achieving objectives
- To allocate resources
- To enable control

Budget cycle

Monitoring/ control action → Objectives → Potential strategies → Evaluate options → Choose strategy → Plans & standards → Budgets → Implementation → Monitoring/ control action

Budgetary process

Step **1** Determine principal budget factor or limiting factor – usually sales – and prepare budget based on forecast sales volume x forecast sales price

Step **2** Prepare budgets for production – volume + costs – and expenses based on volumes used in sales budgets

Step **3** Co-ordinate and review all budgets, then amalgamate in **master budget**

Types of budget/budgeting

- *Flexible budgets*: adjusting the period's budget to reflect actual level of activity
- *Rolling budgets*: updating the budget each month to reflect expenditure
- Incremental budgeting: using past experience as the basis for the current year's budget eg 'last year's sales plus 5%'
- Zero-based budgeting: stating with a blank piece of paper each year so each activity is fully justified before resources are allocated to them

7 Measuring performance – see Chapter 8

8 Strategic management accounting

Providing financial analysis of the business's product markets and competitors' cost structures; monitoring the business's and its competitors' strategies in the market over time; monitoring achievement of competitive advantage.

The finance function must establish adequate *financial control processes*, a form of internal control, in the business.

Internal control

A process designed to provide reasonable assurance as to:
- The effectiveness and efficiency of *operations*
- The reliability of *financial reporting*
- *Compliance* with laws and regulations (COSO)

Control environment

- Provides discipline and structure

Risk assessment

EFFECTIVE INTERNAL CONTROL

Information and communications

- Internal
- External

Monitoring

Control activities

- Approval
- Authorisation
- Verification
- Reconciliation
- Review of operating performance
- Security of assets
- Segregation of duties

8: Measuring performance

Topic List

- Measuring performance
- Profitability measures
- Liquidity/solvency measures
- Efficiency/working capital measures
- Investor measures
- SBU performance
- Balanced scorecard

The finance function plays a key role in providing information for the calculation of performance measures for both internal and external users.

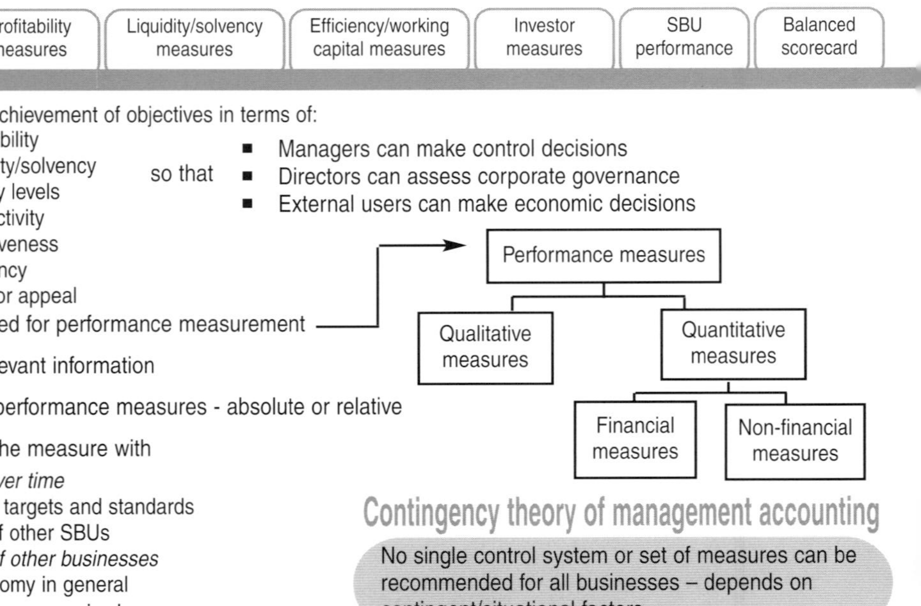

Contingency theory of management accounting

No single control system or set of measures can be recommended for all businesses – depends on contingent/situational factors.

Limitations of performance measures

- Identifying trends + making comparisons
- Timelines and appropriate use of data

Calculate variance of actual from budget/standard

- Volume
- Prices/rates
- Usage
- Efficiency

FINANCIAL MEASURES

- Working capital ratios
- Cash flow
- EPS
- Share price
- Variance analysis
- Revenue targets
- Market share targets
- Customer profitability analysis
- Profit and margins
- ROI and RI
- Labour rates

NON-FINANCIAL MEASURES

- Customer returns
- Enquiries
- Customer satisfaction
- Late deliveries
- Quality
- Labour turnover
- Labour skills
- Production performance
- Innovation

A combination of the two types is best.

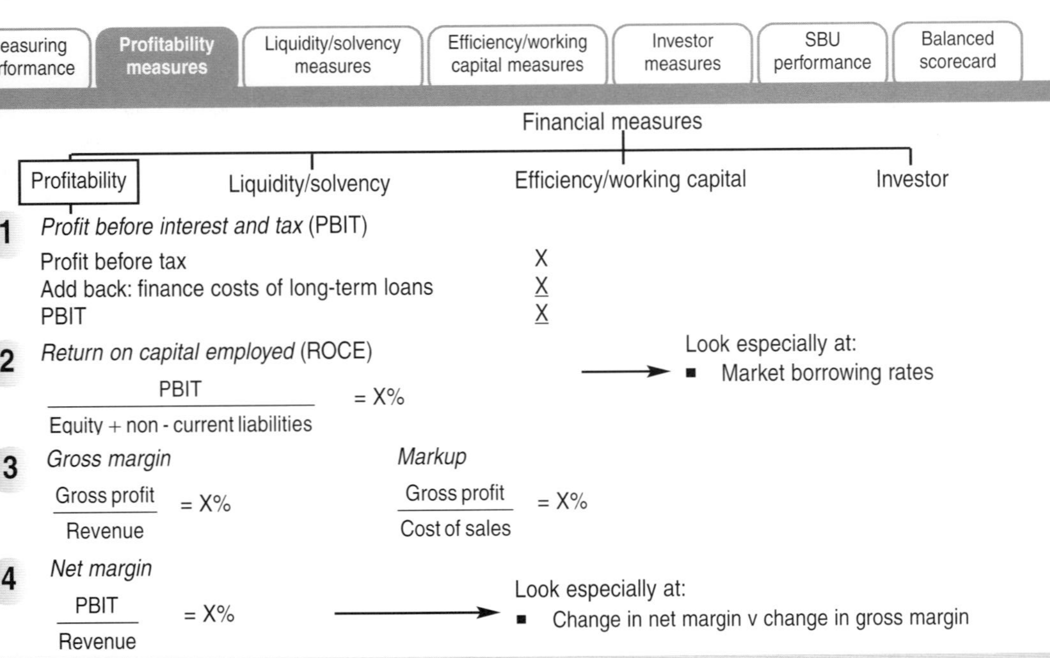

Measuring performance
Profitability measures
Liquidity/solvency measures
Efficiency/working capital measures
Investor measures
SBU performance
Balanced scorecard
Financial measures
Profitability
Liquidity/solvency
Efficiency/working capital
Investor
1 Profit before interest and tax (PBIT)
Profit before tax X
Add back: finance costs of long-term loans X
PBIT X
2 Return on capital employed (ROCE)
PBIT / Equity + non - current liabilities = X%
Look especially at:
■ Market borrowing rates
3 Gross margin
Gross profit / Revenue = X%
Markup
Gross profit / Cost of sales = X%
4 Net margin
PBIT / Revenue = X%
Look especially at:
■ Change in net margin v change in gross margin

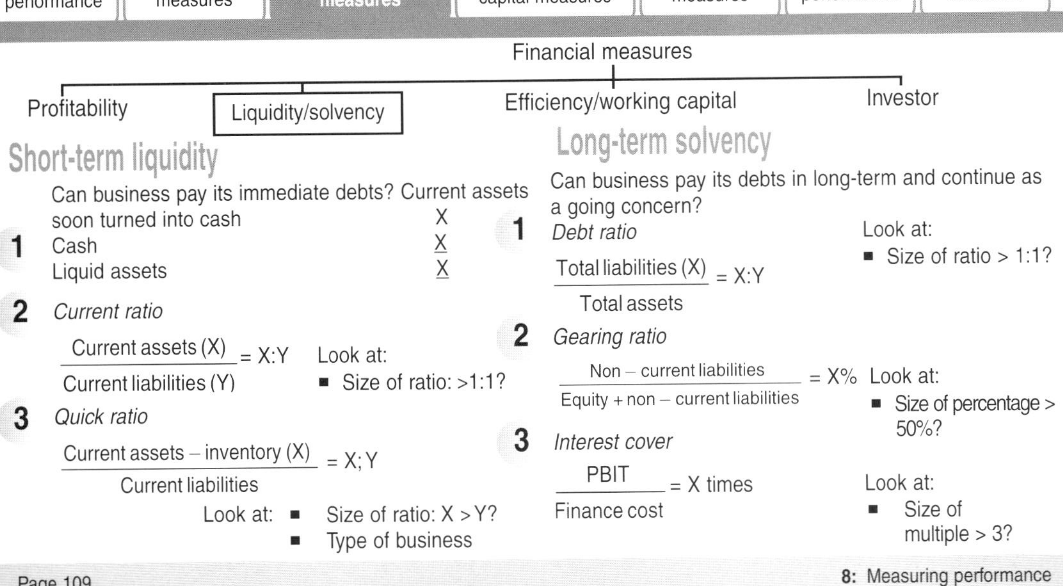

Short-term liquidity

Can business pay its immediate debts? Current assets soon turned into cash

1

Current assets	X
Cash	X
Liquid assets	X

2 *Current ratio*

$$\frac{\text{Current assets (X)}}{\text{Current liabilities (Y)}} = X:Y$$

Look at:

- Size of ratio: >1:1?

3 *Quick ratio*

$$\frac{\text{Current assets} - \text{inventory (X)}}{\text{Current liabilities}} = X;Y$$

Look at:

- Size of ratio: X > Y?
- Type of business

Long-term solvency

Can business pay its debts in long-term and continue as a going concern?

1 *Debt ratio*

$$\frac{\text{Total liabilities (X)}}{\text{Total assets}} = X:Y$$

Look at:

- Size of ratio > 1:1?

2 *Gearing ratio*

$$\frac{\text{Non} - \text{current liabilities}}{\text{Equity} + \text{non} - \text{current liabilities}} = X\%$$

Look at:

- Size of percentage > 50%?

3 *Interest cover*

$$\frac{\text{PBIT}}{\text{Finance cost}} = X \text{ times}$$

Look at:

- Size of multiple > 3?

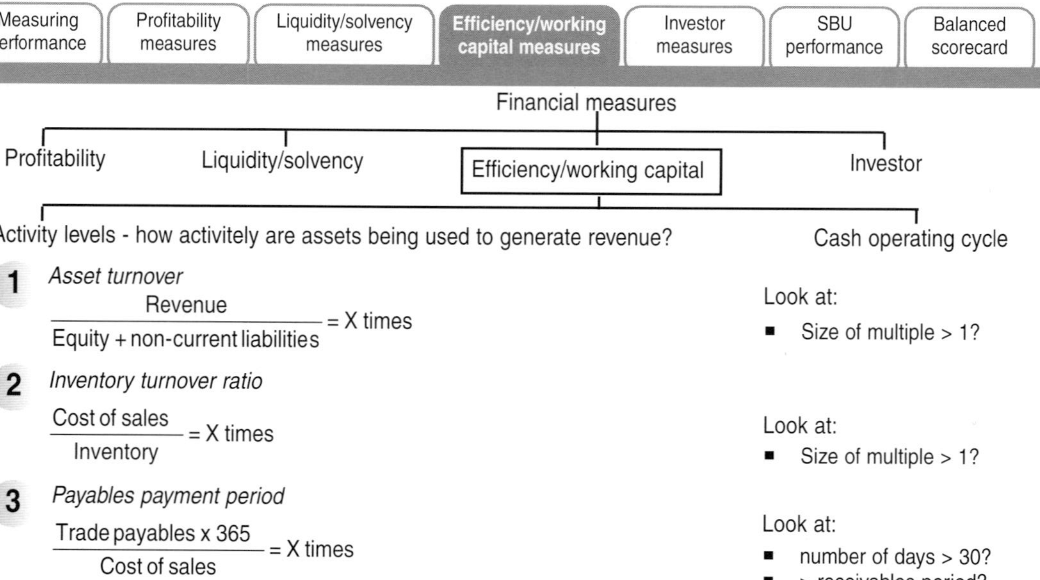

Measuring performance
Profitability measures
Liquidity/solvency measures
Efficiency/working capital measures
Investor measures
SBU performance
Balanced scorecard
Financial measures
Profitability
Liquidity/solvency
Efficiency/working capital
Investor
Activity levels - how activitely are assets being used to generate revenue?
Cash operating cycle
1 Asset turnover
$\frac{\text{Revenue}}{\text{Equity + non-current liabilities}}$ = X times
Look at:
■ Size of multiple > 1?
2 Inventory turnover ratio
$\frac{\text{Cost of sales}}{\text{Inventory}}$ = X times
Look at:
■ Size of multiple > 1?
3 Payables payment period
$\frac{\text{Trade payables x 365}}{\text{Cost of sales}}$ = X times
Look at:
■ number of days > 30?
■ > receivables period?

4 *Inventory turnover period*

$$\frac{\text{Inventory x 365}}{\text{Cost of sales}} = \text{X days}$$

Look at:

- Number of days - as low as possible

5 *Receivables collection period*

$$\frac{\text{Trade receivables x 365}}{\text{Revenue}} = \text{X days}$$

Look at:

- Number of days < 30?

Cash operating cycle

Measures the period of time in days between paying out cash for inputs and receiving cash from customers

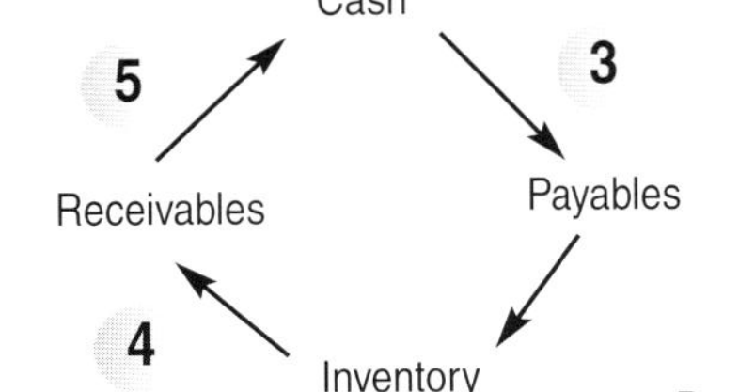

	Days
Inventory turnover period	X
Receivables collection period	X
Payables payment period	(X)
Cash operating cycle	X

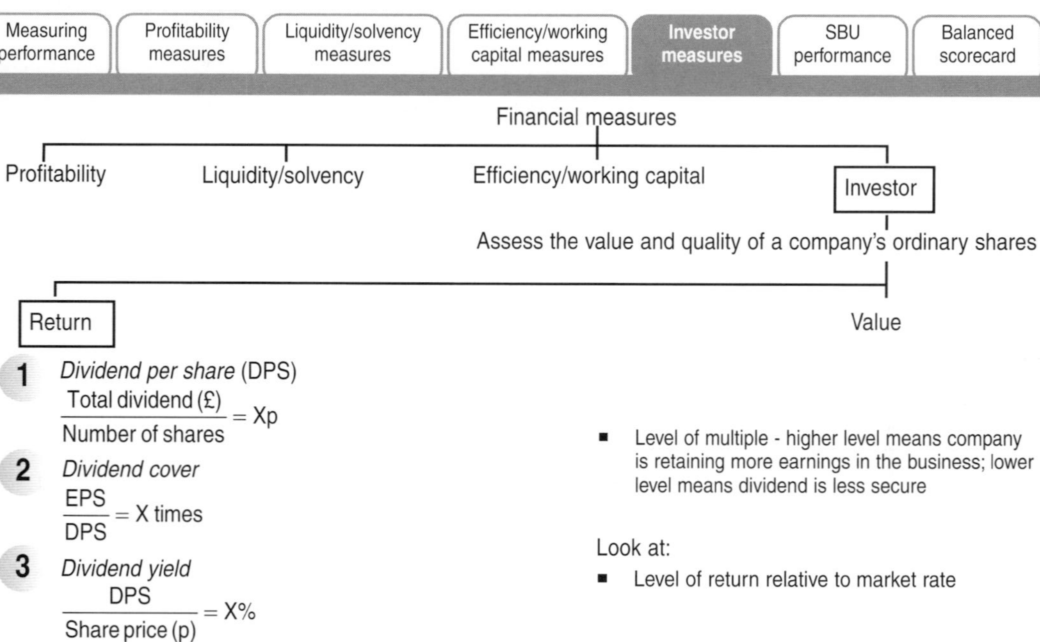

1 *Dividend per share* (DPS)

$$\frac{\text{Total dividend (£)}}{\text{Number of shares}} = \text{Xp}$$

2 *Dividend cover*

$$\frac{\text{EPS}}{\text{DPS}} = \text{X times}$$

- Level of multiple - higher level means company is retaining more earnings in the business; lower level means dividend is less secure

3 *Dividend yield*

$$\frac{\text{DPS}}{\text{Share price (p)}} = \text{X\%}$$

Look at:

- Level of return relative to market rate

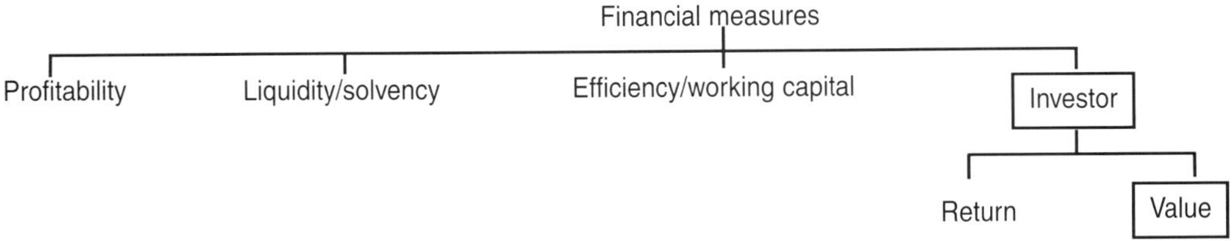

Financial measures

- Profitability
- Liquidity/solvency
- Efficiency/working capital
- Investor
  - Return
  - Value

1 Calculate *earnings per share : EPS* (earnings attributable to each ordinary share) = Xp

2 Establish market price per share

3 Price/earnings ratio : *P/E ratio*

$$\frac{\text{Share price (X)}}{\text{EPS} \quad \text{(Y)}} = X : Y$$

Look at:
- size of ratio – 10 = high investor confidence
- other companies in section
- other companies generally

Often a business seeks to measure the performance of its separate strategic business units (SBUs), using ROI (a relative measure), and RI or EVA® (absolute measures).

Return on investment (ROI)

This is a form of return on capital employed

$$\frac{\text{SBU PBIT}}{\text{Capital employed in SBU}} = X\%$$

Residual income (RI)

This is a measure of the SBU's profits **after deducting an imputed interest cost for the capital used**. RI will increase when investments are made that have returns higher than the business's minimum expectation.

Economic value added (EVA)®

A measure of true economic profit net of the cost of capital used:

PBIT	X
Tax	(X)
Net operating profit after tax (NOPAT)	X
Capital used x cost of capital	(X)
EVA	X

Traditional accounting measures are inadequate for assessing overall progress. Other matters must be considered, especially as financial reporting is heavily retrospective in focus. The **balanced scorecard** covers most of the angles with its four **perspectives**. Note that individual measures are **company specific.**

Customer perspective

'How do customers see us?' This perspective concentrates on customers' concern with time, quality, performance and service. Example measures would be percentage of on-time deliveries and customer rejection rates.

Internal business perspective

'What must we excel at?' This perspective focuses on what the company must be internally to meet its customers' expectations. Control measures will focus on core competence, skills, productivity and cost, for example.

Innovation and learning perspective

'Can we continue to improve and create value?' This perspective is forward looking and concentrates on what the company must do to satisfy future needs. Performance measures include time-to-market for new products and percentage of revenue from them.

Financial perspective

'How do we appear to shareholders?' This is the traditional reporting perspective, but includes ROI, RI and EVA®. Market share and sales growth are included here.

Notes

9: Working capital and treasury management

Topic List

Working capital management

Managing inventory

Managing trade payables

Managing trade receivables

Treasury management

The management of working capital components – inventory, payables, receivables, cash – is a very important part of managing a business's finances.

Treasury management relates specifically to the management of the business's cash.

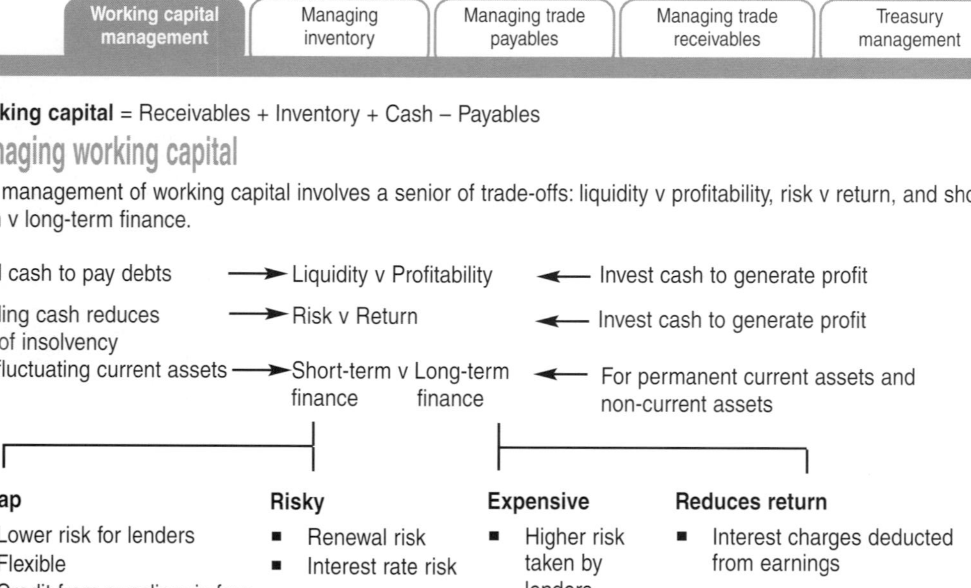

Working capital management
Managing inventory
Managing trade payables
Managing trade receivables
Treasury management
Working capital = Receivables + Inventory + Cash – Payables
Managing working capital
The management of working capital involves a senior of trade-offs: liquidity v profitability, risk v return, and short-term v long-term finance.
Hold cash to pay debts
Liquidity v Profitability
Invest cash to generate profit
Holding cash reduces risk of insolvency
Risk v Return
Invest cash to generate profit
For fluctuating current assets
Short-term finance v Long-term finance
For permanent current assets and non-current assets
Cheap
Lower risk for lenders
Flexible
Credit from suppliers is free
Risky
Renewal risk
Interest rate risk
Expensive
Higher risk taken by lenders
Reduces return
Interest charges deducted from earnings

Financing working capital

	Aggressive	Average	Defensive
Non-current assets	Equity	Equity	Equity
Current assets	Current liabilities	Non-current liabilities Current liabilities	Non-current liability Current liabilities
Profit	High	Medium	Low
Risk	High	Medium	Low

Financing growth

Increased sales = increased inventory and receivables ie increased working capital

To grow without issuing new long term equity/loans, the company must:

- increase profitability and/or
- make better use of assets

Increased investment in working capital increases risk. It also increases the chance of overtrading:

- lengthened cash operating cycle ⇒ more cash required

Overtrading in new businesses:

- No trading record, so less credit from suppliers
- No reputation so longer credit periods for customers
- Niche market = rapid sales expansion

Working capital decisions

When deciding whether to invest or reduce working capital, the business can:

- manipulate ratios to see effect of decision on risk/return
- calculate revised cash operating cycles to see effect on liquidity
- look at ratios/cycles used by similar companies

Solving liquidity problems

- Reduce inventory-holding period
- Reduce production period
- Reduce credit period for customers
- Improve cash collection
- Extend credit period from supplies (pay later)

Inventory

- Raw materials and components
- Spare parts/consumables
- Work-in-progress
- Finished goods
- Goods purchased for resale

Uses up cash but generates returns
Liquidity v Profitability

Reasons for holding inventory

- Buffer to meet demand
- Avoid risk of stockouts
- Avoid reliance on supplier lead times
- Ensure continuity of production
- Take advantage of quantity discounts and special promotions
- Buy at low price ahead of rises
- Order infrequently ⇒ reduced ordering costs
- Seasonality of demand
- Suppliers insist on minimum order quantities

Inventory costs

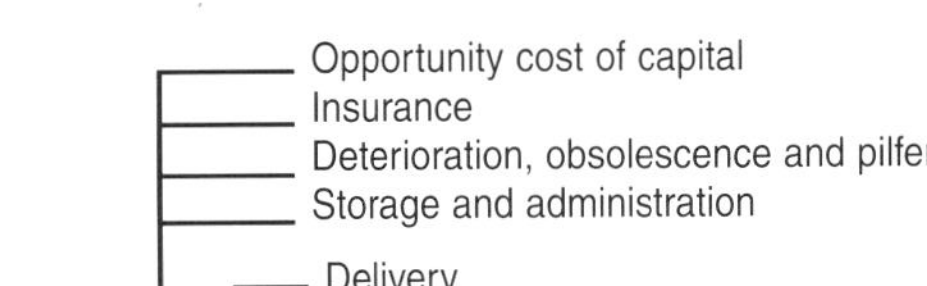
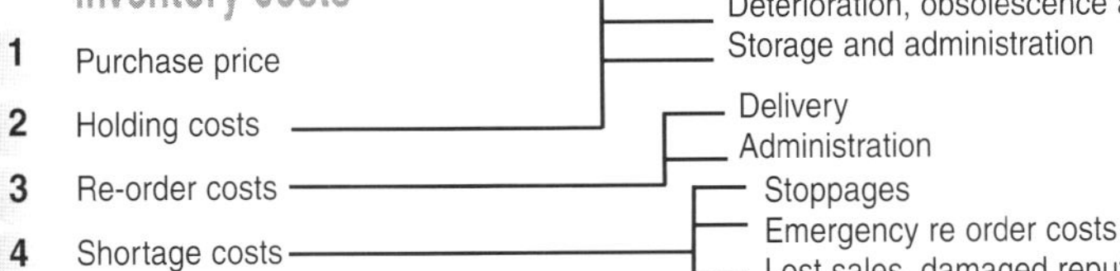

1. Purchase price
2. Holding costs
   - Opportunity cost of capital
   - Insurance
   - Deterioration, obsolescence and pilferage
   - Storage and administration
3. Re-order costs
   - Delivery
   - Administration
4. Shortage costs
   - Stoppages
   - Emergency re order costs
   - Lost sales, damaged reputation

Inventory control systems

- *Re-order level system* – the optimum quantity is ordered once inventory level reaches a certain level eg two-bin system
- *Periodic review system* – levels are reviewed at certain points in time, and a variable amount is reordered at each point
- *ABC system* – A – high value/importance, closely monitored
  B – lower value/importance, less frequently monitored
  C – least important, not closely monitored
- *Economic order quantity (EOQ)* – calculates how much to order and when, taking into account:
  c – cost of placing one order
  d – estimated usage over a particular period
  h – cost of holding one unit for that period

$$EOQ = \sqrt{\frac{2cd}{h}}$$

- *Just-in-time system* – deliveries flow straight through to production/resale, so minimum inventory is held. Requires flexibility, quality, close relations with with suppliers and rationalised layouts
- *Perpetual inventory* – inventory movement in and out monitored on computer, with re-orders triggered automatically (expert system)

Avdvantages of trade credit

- Convenient and informal
- Low cost
- Available to most businesses
- Settlement discount may be available
- Provides subsidy for new products
- Flexible in short-term

But taking too long to pay suppliers has costs:

- damaged credit status
- raised prices to compensate suppliers
- loss of discount for early payment

Improving payables management

- Weigh up value of credit period v value of settlement discounts
- Negotiate better terms for large quantities
- Reconcile suppliers' statements carefully
- Pay only once delivery is complete
- Look for improved terms and consider switching

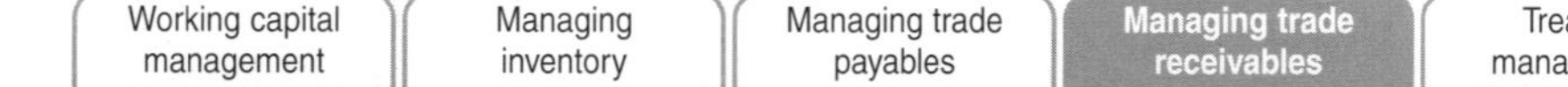

TRADE-OFFS RE GRANTING CREDIT TO CUSTOMERS

COSTS

- **Financing costs** → Shorten cash cycle
- **Irrecoverable debts** → Avoid bad debts
- Administration

v

BENEFITS

- Increased sales
- Larger profits

Grant credit to customers?

Credit rating

Determines whether/how much credit should be extended to a customer. Consider:

- ability of customer to pay
- analysis of financial statements
- using credit rating agencies
- trading experience with customer
- credit limits
- references

Credit terms and settlement discounts

Influenced by trade custom:

- **Credit period** eg 30 days credit
- **Settlement discount** eg 2% discount for payment within 10 days

Collection procedures should ensure customers pay within credit period

Calculate:

- cost of discount v benefit of quicker receipt
- effect on cash flows
- effect on profit (reduced irrecoverable debts)

To receive its cash from sales earlier, the business could use invoice discounting or receivables factoring.

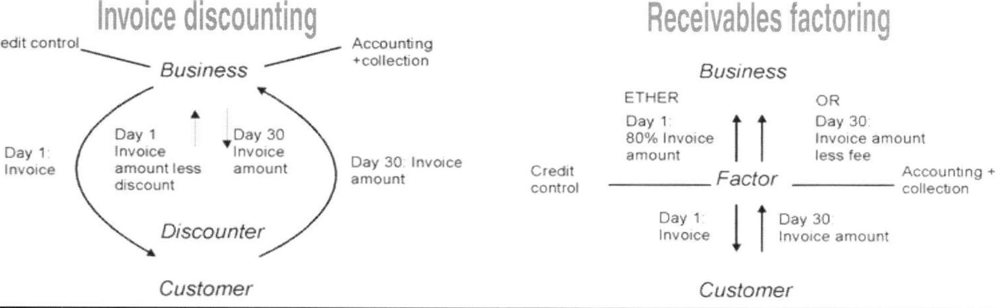

Managing recevables well

- Key accounts: 20: 80 rule
- Reduce order → sale time
- Invoice immediately/send credit notes promptly
- Reduce invoice → collection time: monitor receivables ageing
- Personal contract
- Link sales commission to cash received, not invoices
- Set targets
- Take out credit insurance

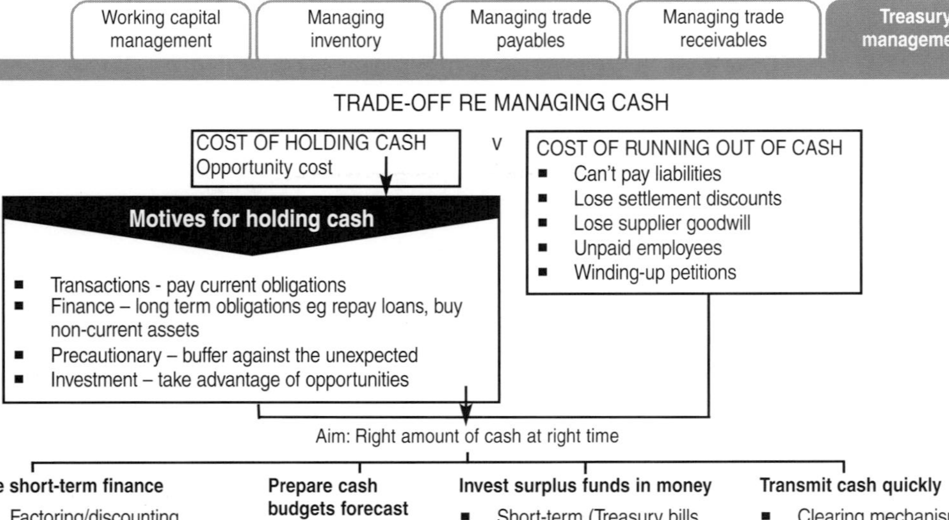
TRADE-OFF RE MANAGING CASH
COST OF HOLDING CASH
Opportunity cost
v
COST OF RUNNING OUT OF CASH
■ Can't pay liabilities
■ Lose settlement discounts
■ Lose supplier goodwill
■ Unpaid employees
■ Winding-up petitions
Motives for holding cash
■ Transactions - pay current obligations
■ Finance – long term obligations eg repay loans, buy non-current assets
■ Precautionary – buffer against the unexpected
■ Investment – take advantage of opportunities
Aim: Right amount of cash at right time
Use short-term finance
■ Factoring/discounting
■ Use overdrafts
■ Use short-term loans
■ Operating leases
Prepare cash budgets forecast
Invest surplus funds in money
■ Short-term (Treasury bills, deposits, gilts, bonds, equities)
■ Long-term (projects)
Transmit cash quickly
■ Clearing mechanisms
– cheque clearing
– CHAPS
– BACS
■ Banking procedures

The banking system

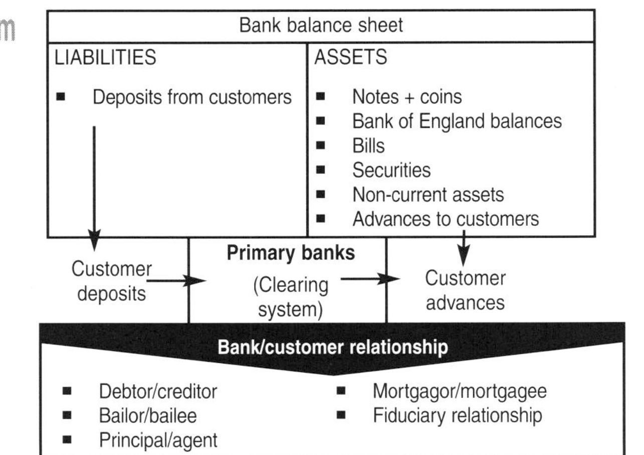

Bank's duties

- Honour customer's cheques
- Credit funds to customer's account
- Repay funds on demand
- Comply with customer's instructions
- Provide statements
- Respect confidentiality

Bank's rights

- Reasonable charges
- Use funds
- Receive repayment of overdraft on demand
- Indemnity from customer

Customer's duties

- Exercise care
- Tell bank of known forgeries

Capital markets

- **London Stock Exchange**:
  1. **Main market**, with firm regulation, for raising funds through new issues of shares (primary market), and trading existing shares (secondary market).
  2. **Alternative Investment Market:** for newer companies, less firmly regulated.
- **Gilt edged market** for UK government stock
- **International capital markets** are operated between banks in larger countries to provide major finance for very large companies and institutions. Confusingly, their securities are known as eurobonds.
- Certain stocks not traded on recognised stock exchanges are traded in **over the counter** markets.

Money markets

Short-term investment and borrowing of funds is handled in the **money markets**. These are operated by the banks and other financial institutions and include markets for:

- Certificates of deposit
- Bills of exchange and commercial paper
- Treasury bills
- Building society bulk borrowing
- Local authority bills and other short-term borrowing

Notes

10: The professional accountant

Topic List

- The accountancy profession
- The professional accountant
- Professional responsibility, ethics & principles
- Accounting principles
- Accounting standards

In this chapter we look at the purpose, importance and work of the accountancy profession, at the requirements; for technical competence and professional responsibility from professional accountants, at the roles accountants play in society, and at the purpose and uses of accounting principles and standards.

Purpose of the accountancy profession

To provide support to users of information making resource allocation decisions

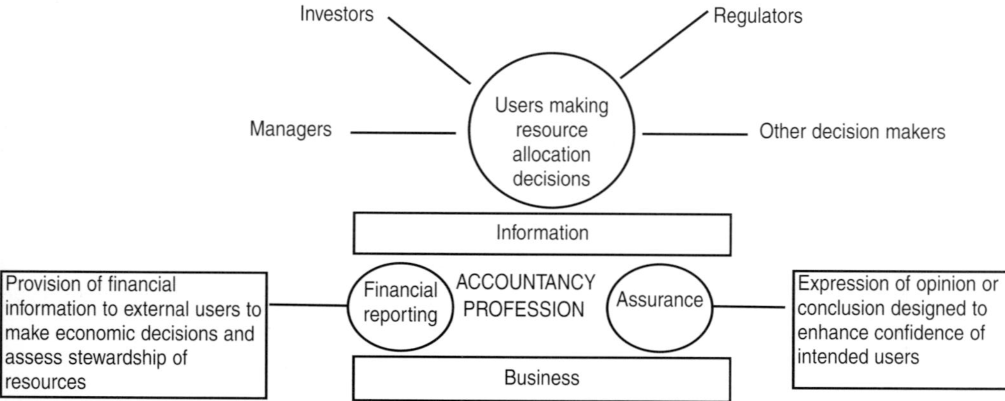

Importance of profession

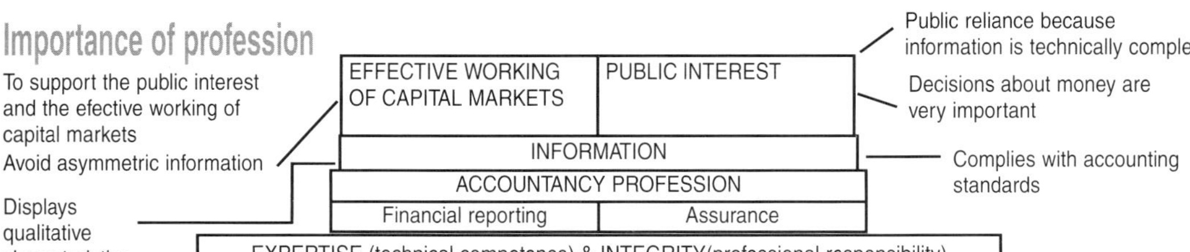

Work of the professional accountant

Per Professional Oversight Board (POB):

1 Maintaining control and safeguarding assets

- Complete, timely, accurate, transactions recording
- Sufficient internal controls
- Properly constituted + informed audit committee
- Qualified and resourced non-executive directors

Financial management

2 Raising and using financial resources

- New finance
- Using funds to achieve objectives
- Planning control
- Treasury management
- Risk management

3 Financial reporting

- Apply professional principles
- Apply accounting principles

The professional accountant requires **technical competence** and **professional responsibility**.

Technical competence

This is assured by:

1 *Entry and education requirements of ICAEW*

- ≥ 2 A levels
- 3 year training contract
- Course of theoretical instruction
- PASS ICAEW exams
- Certificate of suitability
- Pay admission + subscription fees

→
- Knowledge and understanding
- Skills and abilities
- Personal commitment and professional principles

\+

2 *Requirements for continuing membership of ICAEW*

FOR ALL MEMBERS

- Obey rules + regulations
- Pay annual subscription fee
- Undertake Continuing Professional Education (CPE)

FOR MEMBERS IN PUBLIC PRACTICE

Plus
- Practising certificate
- Implement Code of Ethics
- Have professional indemnity insurance (PII)

\+

3 *Requirement for ICAEW members in reserved areas*

- Statutory audit
- Investment business
- Insolvency

Comply with regulations set by ICAEW or recognised professional regulator on eligibilty, conduct and competence

Roles of the professional acountant

In practice		In business
RESERVED AREAS	NON-RESERVED AREAS	■ Wide number of business areas ■ Wide number of roles ■ Roles/responsibilities limited by requirement to act with professional competence and due care
■ Investment business ■ Insolvency ■ Audit	■ Accounting ■ Tax ■ Management consulting ■ Financial management ■ Corporate finance ■ ICT ■ Forensic accounting	

Must be:

- Member of recognised supervisory body eg ICAEW
- Appropriately qualified

May be:

- Sole practitioner, partnership or LLP

May NOT be:

- Officer/employee of company
- Partner/employee of such a person

ICAEW's **Code of Ethics** stresses the importance of the public interest, and of **public trust** in the profession. It sets out:

1. Fundamental principles
2. A conceptual framework (see *Assurance*)
3. Threats to compliance
4. Safeguards

Fundamental principles

Integrity	*Objectivity*	*Professional competence /due care*	*Confidentiality*	*Professional behaviour*
✓ Straightforward ✓ Honest ✓ Fair ✓ Truthful × Self-interest × Undue influence × Reckless × False/misleading	✓ Independent of mind × Bias × Conflict of interest × Undue influence	✓ Appropriate knowledge + skill ✓ Sound + independent judgement ✓ Diligence – careful, thorough, timely ✓ Technical/professional standards ✓ Distinction between expression of opinion + assertion of fact	✓ All unpublished information on employer/client is confidential ✓ Actively preserve confidentiality × Disclosure × Personal advantage	✓ Compliance with laws/regulations ✓ Courtesy ✓ Consideration ✓ Honesty ✓ Truthfulness × Actions that discredit profession × Exaggerated claims × Disparaging references to fellow professionals

1 Identify threats to compliance

Self-interest threat

Accountant's own financial interests dominate

Self-review threat

Accountant reevaluates a previous judgement made by him/herself.

Advocacy threat

Accountant promotes a position/opinion so hard he/she is no longer objective

Familiarity threat

Accountant is too sympathetic to a particular group with which he/she has a close relationship

Intimidation threat

Accountant is deterred from acting by actual or peceived threat

2 Implement safeguards

Professional safeguards

- Entry/education requirements of ICAEW
- CPE
- Professional standards
- Professional monitoring
- Disciplinary procedures
- External review by third party
- Corporate governance
- Complaints systems
- Duty to report ethics breaches

Workplace safeguards

- Vary from place to place

Use of accounting principles

To inform profesional judgements in financial reporting

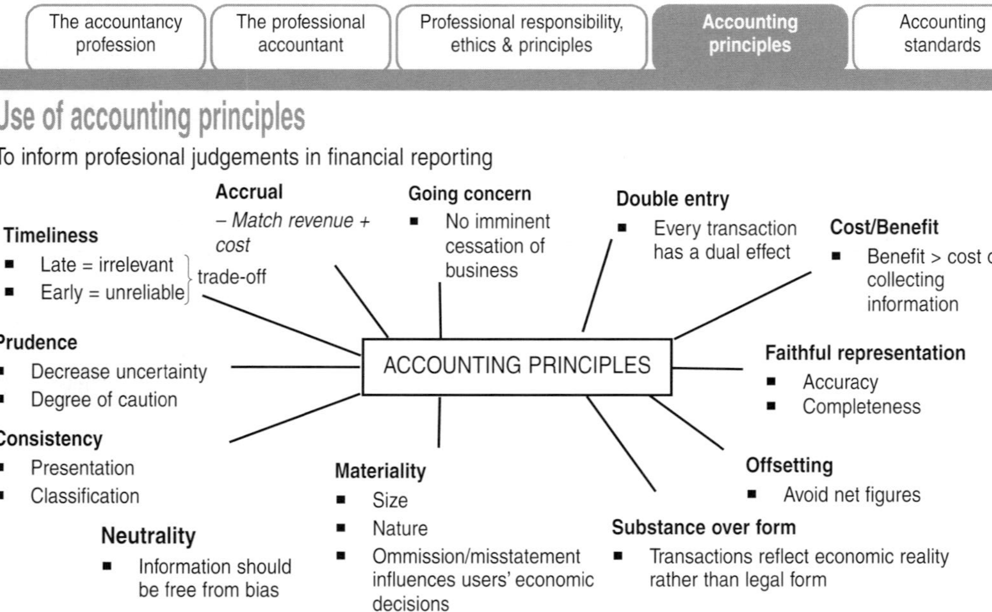

Purpose of accounting standards

To identify proper accounting practice for preparers, auditiors + users of financial statements

Types of accounting standards

International - for all UK companies by 2008

- IASs
- IFRSs
- Issued by IASB

Converging ←

UK

- SSAPs
- FRSs
- Issued by ASB

UK GAAP

- Accounting standards + practice
  PLUS
- Companies Act
  – reporting requirements
  – accounting records
  – statutory audit

Standard-setting process

1 Study national requirements/practice
2 Discussion with national standardsetters
3 Consult SAC
4 Issue Discussion Paper
5 Issue Exposure Draft (ED)
6 Consider comments on ED
7 Conduct public hearing/field tests
8 Publish standard

Compulsory steps: 3, 5, 6, 8

11: Structure and regulation of the accountancy profession

Topic List

While the ICAEW regulates its members. The profession itself is self-regulating. This incorporates a degree of oversight by the FRC's Professional Oversight Board (POB).

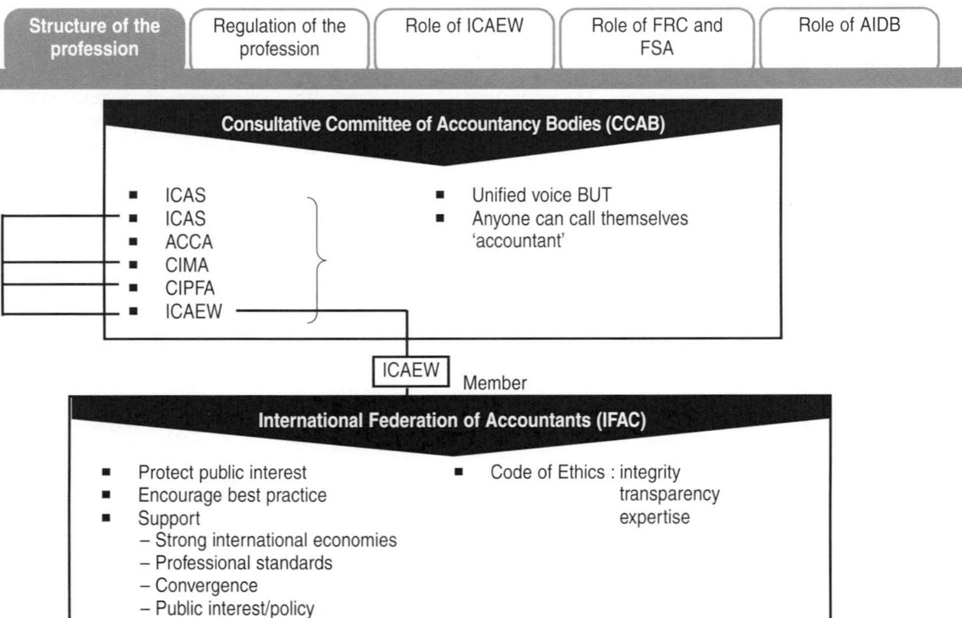

Structure of the profession
Regulation of the profession
Role of ICAEW
Role of FRC and FSA
Role of AIDB
Consultative Committee of Accountancy Bodies (CCAB)
ICAS
ICAS
ACCA
CIMA
CIPFA
ICAEW
Unified voice BUT
Anyone can call themselves 'accountant'
AAT
ICAEW
Member
International Federation of Accountants (IFAC)
Protect public interest
Encourage best practice
Support
– Strong international economies
– Professional standards
– Convergence
– Public interest/policy
Code of Ethics : integrity
transparency
expertise

Methods of regulation

- Legislation by government
- Delegated legislation via agencies
- Self regulation by profession, plus **oversight mechanism**
- Combination

Requires

- Sufficient independence from profession
- Knowledge
- Input profession
- Balance of stakeholder interests
- Authority
- Good communication
- Resources

Regulation of accountancy profession

- Government legislation
- Regulation by FRC
- Self-regulation + oversight by POB

Aims of oversight mechanism

- *Protect public interest* from:
  – being misled
  – abuse of power through asymmetric information/monopoly
- Facilitate competition/reduce trade barriers
- Ensure high technical, ethical and educational standards
- Flexibility
- Transparency 'justice is seen to be done'
- Fairness

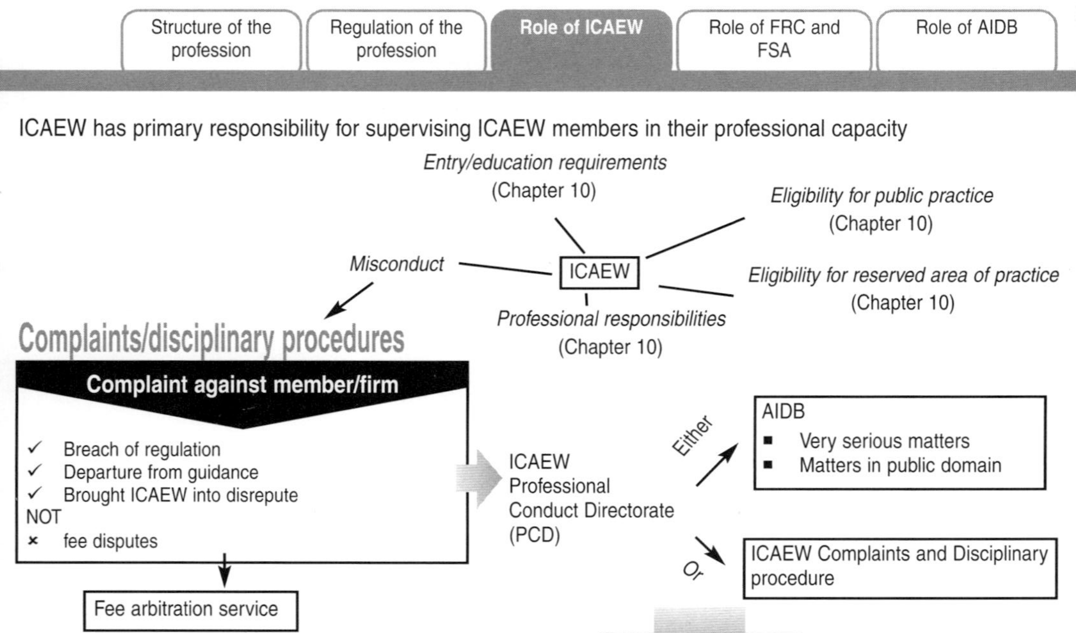

Structure of the profession
Regulation of the profession
Role of ICAEW
Role of FRC and FSA
Role of AIDB
ICAEW has primary responsibility for supervising ICAEW members in their professional capacity
Entry/education requirements (Chapter 10)
Eligibility for public practice (Chapter 10)
Eligibility for reserved area of practice (Chapter 10)
Professional responsibilities (Chapter 10)
ICAEW
Misconduct
Complaints/disciplinary procedures
Complaint against member/firm
✓ Breach of regulation
✓ Departure from guidance
✓ Brought ICAEW into disrepute
NOT
× fee disputes
Fee arbitration service
ICAEW Professional Conduct Directorate (PCD)
Either
AIDB
Very serious matters
Matters in public domain
Or
ICAEW Complaints and Disciplinary procedure

ICAEW complaints & disciplinary procedure

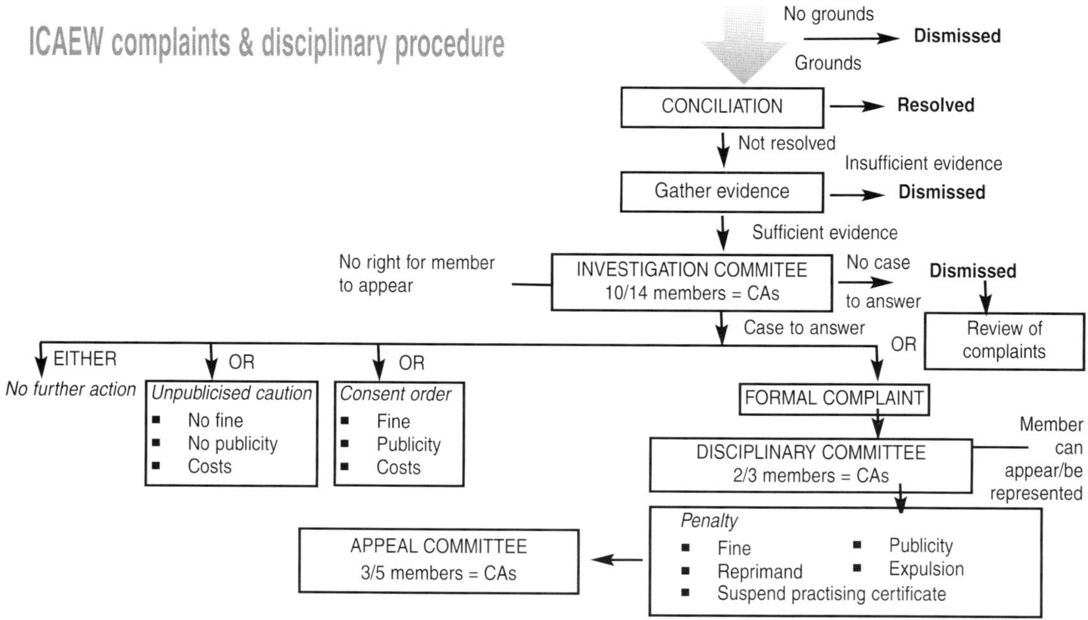

No grounds → **Dismissed**

Grounds

CONCILIATION → **Resolved**

Not resolved

Gather evidence → Insufficient evidence → **Dismissed**

Sufficient evidence

INVESTIGATION COMMITEE
10/14 members = CAs

No right for member to appear

No case to answer → **Dismissed** → Review of complaints

Case to answer

EITHER
No further action

OR
Unpublicised caution
- No fine
- No publicity
- Costs

OR
Consent order
- Fine
- Publicity
- Costs

OR
FORMAL COMPLAINT

DISCIPLINARY COMMITTEE
2/3 members = CAs

Member can appear/be represented

Penalty
- Fine
- Reprimand
- Suspend practising certificate
- Publicity
- Expulsion

APPEAL COMMITTEE
3/5 members = CAs

Role of Financial Reporting Committee (FRC)

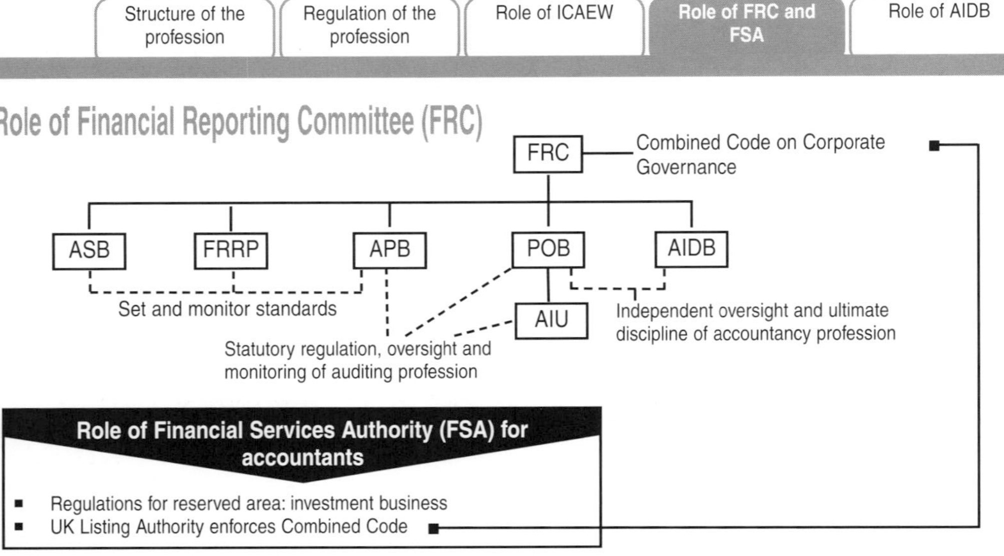

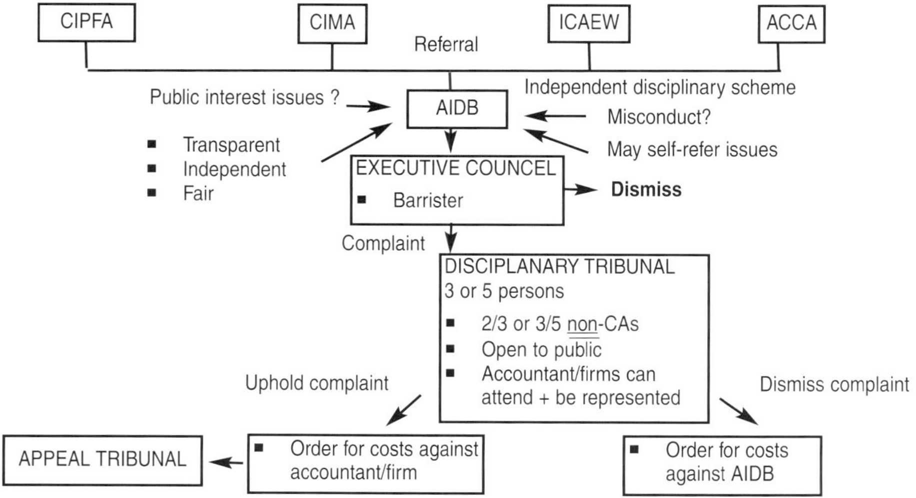

CIPFA | CIMA | ICAEW | ACCA

Referral

AIDB

Public interest issues ?

- Transparent
- Independent
- Fair

Independent disciplinary scheme

Misconduct?

May self-refer issues

EXECUTIVE COUNCEL
- Barrister

Dismiss

Complaint

DISCIPLANARY TRIBUNAL
3 or 5 persons
- 2/3 or 3/5 non-CAs
- Open to public
- Accountant/firms can attend + be represented

Uphold complaint

- Order for costs against accountant/firm

APPEAL TRIBUNAL

Dismiss complaint

- Order for costs against AIDB

12: Governance and ethics

Topic List

- Why is governance an issue?
- Good corporate governance
- Governance structures
- Ethical culture

In this chapter we look at the ideas underlying corporate governance and its structures, and at ethical culture and business values.

Agency theory

Proposes that, whilst individual team members act in their own self-interest, individual well-being depends on the well-being of other individuals and on the performance of the team.

Businesses are set of contracts between principals (suppliers of finance) and agents (directors).

The agency problem

If directors don't have significant shareholdings, they can under-perform and over-reward themselves because

- They have better information
- They are insufficiently accountable

Stakeholder perspective

Directors have a duty of care to the wider community of stakeholders.

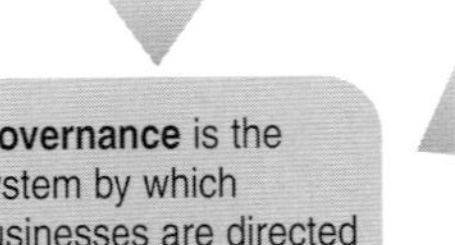

Governance is the system by which businesses are directed and controlled

Corporate perspective

Directors balance shareholder and other linked stakeholder interests to maximise company wealth

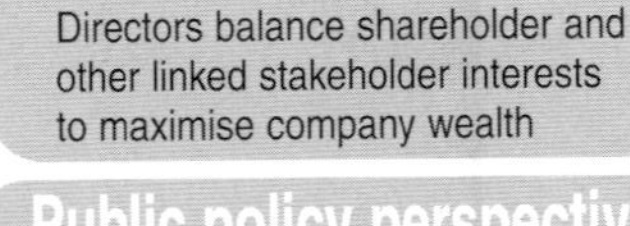

Public policy perspective

As corporate perspective, plus interests of public at large.

Stewardship perspective

Directors have company's best interest at heart; they are the stewards of the asset of the company so shareholders take little or no part in running it.

Internationalisation | Investor treatment | Financial reporting weaknesses | Types of financial systems | Corporate scandals

Corporate governance

Structured system for company's direction and control that

- specifies rights/responsibilities of **stakeholders**
- establishes rules and procedures for decision-making about company

Stakeholder needs

- Company objectives reflect interests/expectations
- Reduced conflicts of interest
- Good corporate governance practice
- Good business ethics

Openness | Transparency | Reduced conflict of interest | Accountability | Reconciled interests

Need alignment of directors' and shareholders' interests.

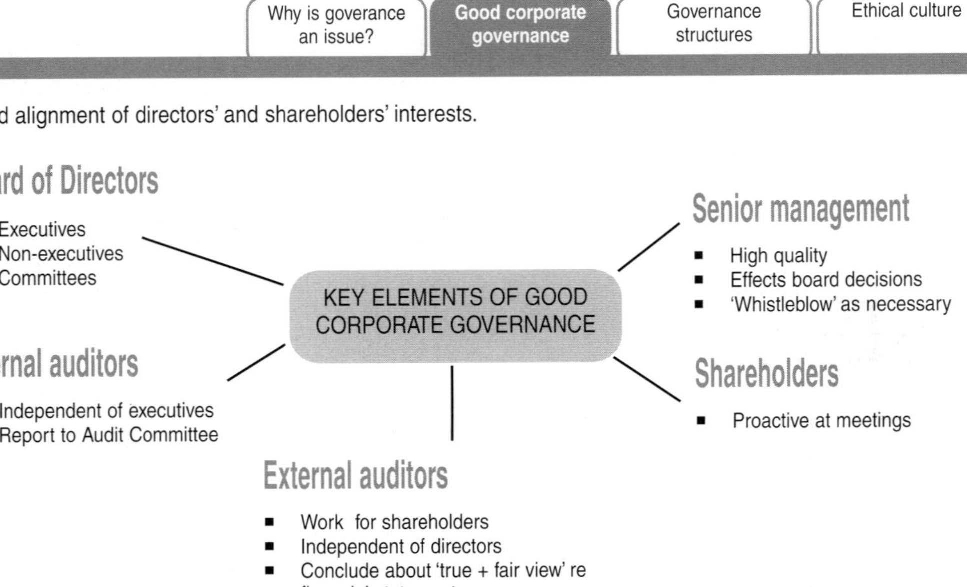

Governance structure

Principles-based approach ← Set of legal or regulatory methods that ensure effective corporate governance. → Shareholder-led approach

OECD principles of corporate governance

Organisation for Economic Co-operation and Development produced non-binding principles to address the interests of global investors. Companies should work towards achieving principles.

OECD Principles

- Transparent and efficient financial markets
- Shareholder/stakeholder rights
- Equitable treatment of all shareholders
- Stakeholders' rights protected
- Timely/accurate disclosure of material matters
- Board responsible for strategy and monitoring
- Board should act with due diligence and in company's best interests

Extend
audit

nalysts

Instutional shareholders

- Insurance companies
- Pension funds
- Investment trusts

Types of financial system

- Bank-based financial system
- Market-based financial system

Structure for board of directors

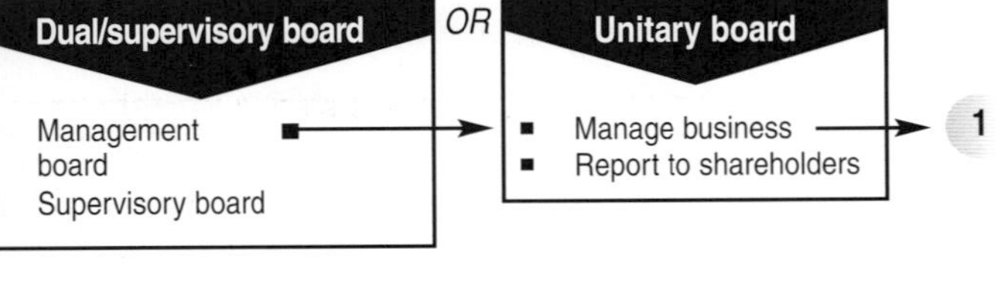

UK governance structure

1 Company law

- Unitary board of directiors
- Directors' powers + duties
- Loans + contracts with directors
- Accountability
- Meetings

2 UKLA rules for listed companies

- Combined Code (Chapter 13)

Ethics

Tell us know to behave

Business ethics

Moral standards expected of a decent company by society

Social responsability

- How for company exceeds minimum expectations of regulation/corporate governance
- Obligations to stakeholders with no contractual business relationship

Ethical culture

Business's basic values and beliefs encourage people to comply with business ethics. Promoted by board of directors

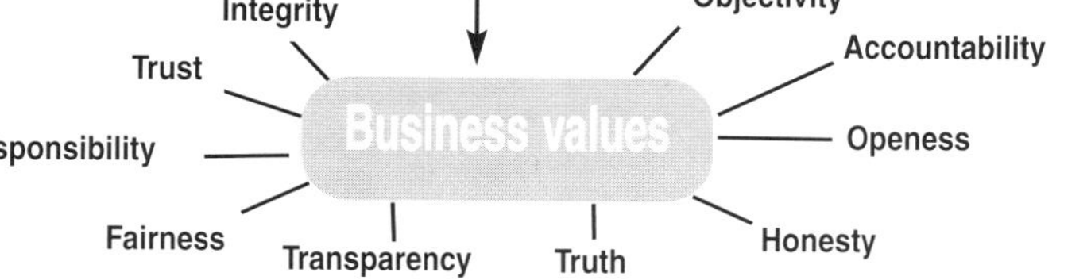

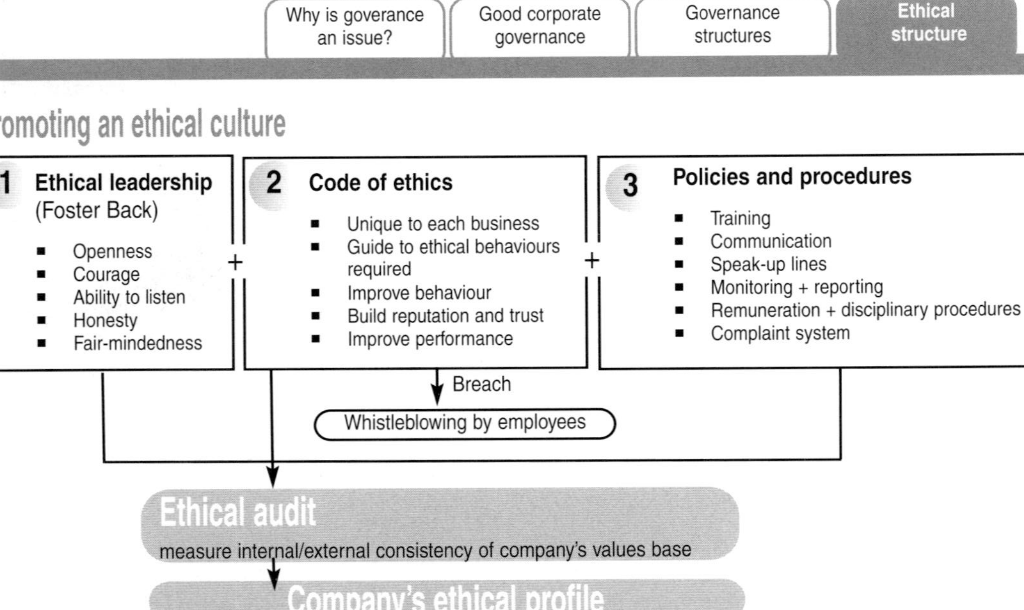
Promoting an ethical culture
1 Ethical leadership
(Foster Back)
Openness
Courage
Ability to listen
Honesty
Fair-mindedness
+
2 Code of ethics
Unique to each business
Guide to ethical behaviours required
Improve behaviour
Build reputation and trust
Improve performance
+
3 Policies and procedures
Training
Communication
Speak-up lines
Monitoring + reporting
Remuneration + disciplinary procedures
Complaint system
Breach
Whistleblowing by employees
Ethical audit
measure internal/external consistency of company's values base
Company's ethical profile

13: Corporate governance

Topic List

In this chapter we look at the details of the Combined Code on Corporate Governance, and the related Turnbull Evidence, issued by the FRC as a voluntary code of practice. For listed UK companies, these are effectively compulsory under the FSA's UKLA.

The **Combined Code** on Corporate Governance is set out in the form of **principles**, with supporting provisions.

Effective board

Every company should be headed by an effective board, which is collectively responsible for the success of the company.

- Board gives entrepreneurial leadership
- Board sets strategic aim, plus values and standards
- Every director has an **active** role in **managing** the company.
- Non-executives are very important

Chairman and Chief Executive

There should be a clear division of responsibilities at the head of the company between running the board (the Chairman) and running the company (Chief Executive).

- Chief Executive and Chairman should be different people
- Chief Executive should not go on to be Chairman on retirement.

Balance and independence

The board should include a balance of executive and non-executive directors...such that no individual/small group dominates.

- There should be **independent** non-executives
- The board should be the right size
- Membership of board committees should regularly be refreshed

Board appointment

There should be a formal, rigorous and transparent procedure for appointment to the board.

A **nomination committee** comprised largely of independent non-executives should be formed.

Information and development

The board should be supplied in a timely manner with information in a form and of a quality appropriate to enable it to discharge its duties.

- All directors should receive induction training on joining the board
- Directors should regularly update and refresh their skills and knowledge

Evaluating performance

The board should undertake formal and rigorous annual evaluations of its performance and that of its committees and individual directors.

- Individual directors to be evaluated
- Chairman to act on identified strengths and weaknesses, handling proposing new members/rejection of weak members.
- Performance evaluation procedure should be discussed in the annual report

Re-election of directors

Directors should be re-elected at regular intervals so there is planned and professional refreshing of the board.

- All directors re-elected every 3 years
- Non-executives serving longer than 6 years should be rigorously reviewed.
- Non-executives serving longer than 9 years subject to annual re-election. Are probably not independent.

Directors' remuneration

Remuneration should be sufficient to attain, retain and motivate directors. Executive remuneration should be linked to corporate and individual performance.

- **Remuneration committee** to monitor levels of remuneration, service contracts and compensation payments.
- Remuneration policy should cover performance related elements, executive share options, and non-executive pay.

Transparency of remuneration

Formal and transparent procedure for developing policy on executive remuneration, and remuneration packages of individual directors. No director should be involved in deciding his/her own remuneration.

- Remuneration committee may consult with Chairman/Chief Executive, but conflicts of interest must be avoided
- Principal shareholders should be consulted
- Remuneration committee to comprise of at least 3 independent non-executives.

Financial reporting

The board should present a balanced and understandable assessment of the company's position and prospects.

- Assessment includes interim reports, price-sensitivity public statements and regulatory reports, as well as annual financial statements
- Directors must state their responsibility for financial statements in the annual report, and that the company is a going concern
- Auditors should explain their responsibilities in the annual report

Internal control

Board should maintain a sound system of internal control to safeguard shareholders' investment and the company's assets.

- Annual review by board of material controls
- See Turnbull Guidance

Auditing

Formal and transparent arrangement for how to apply financial reporting and internal control principles, and for maintaining the appropriate relationship with the company's auditors.

- **Audit committee** of at least 3 independent non-executives, at least 1 with recent and relevant financial experience

AGM

The board should use the AGM to communicate with investors and encourage their participation.

Dialogue with shareholders

Board is responsible for ensuring a dialogue with institutional shareholders based on a mutual understanding of objectives.

Dialogue with companies

Institutional shareholders should have a dialogue with the company based on mutual understanding of objectives.

ISC Statement of Principles

- Shareholder engagement
- Deal effectively with concerns about underperformance

Evaluation of governance disclosures

The company's governance arrangements, especially board structure and composition, should be given due evaluation. Particular attention is due to departures from the Code.

Shareholder voting

Make considered use of votes, and attend AGM

A process designed to provide reasonable assurance regarding the achievement of objectives via:

- effective and efficient operations
- reliable financial reporting
- compliance with laws/regulations

PLUS

Turnbull Guidance

Internal control system:

- Appropriate response to risk
- Safeguard assets
- Identify and manage liabilities
- Reliable internal reporting

Responsibilty of board of directiors for sound system of internal control

- Policy-making for financial, operational and compliance control systems and risk management, taking risk-based approach
- Review system's effectiveness in addressing identified risks
- Annual report on internal control system to shareholders

Statement on internal control

- Acknowledge responsibility
- Manage not eliminate risk
- Reasonable, not absolute assurance
- Ongoing process
- Regular review of systems
- Compliance with Turnbull Guidance

Sound system of internal control does NOT eliminate risk of

- poor judgement in decision making
- human error
- deliberate circumvention of control processes
- management override
- unforeseen circumstances occurring

External audit

Purpose: to issue an opinion in an audit report as to whether the financial statements give a *true and fair view* of the company's financial performance for the period, and of its financial position at the year-end

Additional reports:

- on the director's remuneration report
- on compliance with the Combined Code

Appointment:

- recommended by audit committee and board
- voted on by shareholders

Prevention/detection of fraud and error: NOT responsibility of external auditor

Directors

Must satisfy themselves that the internal control and risk management systems operate effectively → *Managers*: Must implement and monitor these → Internal audit

Internal audit (IA):

Monitors effective operation of internal control and risk management systems

Areas covered by IA

- Operational controls
- Financial controls
- Compliance (financial and non-financial)

Role of Audit Committee

- Appoints head of IA
- Ensures sufficient resources are available for IA

Tasks of IA

Assess:

- risk identification, analysis and management

Advise on:

- embedding risk management processes
- improving internal controls

Ensure:

- safeguarding of assets
- effective and efficient operations
- compliance with laws/regulations
- reliable/accurate records and reports

Help with:

- detection of error/fraud
- identifying savings/opportunities

14: The economic environment of business and finance

Topic List

The economic environment of a business is determined by the forces of supply and demand, and by government regulation.

Economics

the production and consumption of goods and services: what to produce, how to produce it and who to produce it for:

Market economy	—	Mixed economy	—	Command economy
Free markets and private ownership		Market system with some regulation		Government planning and control

The production of goods and services requires the utilisation of economic **resources** or **factors of production**. These resources are **scarce** and therefore choices must be made to how they are to be employed.

- **LAND** includes all **natural resources**. Land itself is limited in quantity but can be improved in quality.
- **LABOUR** is people employed to produce goods and services. it varies in quality.
- **CAPITAL** consists of physical goods that aid production. Money can be transformed into capital.
- **ENTERPRISE** is needed both to organise production and to take the risk of possible financial loss.

A market

Potential buyers and potential sellers come together for the purpose of exchange.

Market structure

The number of buyers and sellers in a market and their relative bargaining power.

The Firm

Sellers are **firms**. Buyers of consumer goods and services are **households.**

Micro-economic environment

How the market mechanism of the interaction of supply and demand for an item affects a particular firm

Macro-economic environment

The world in which all firms operate, incorporating global and national influences

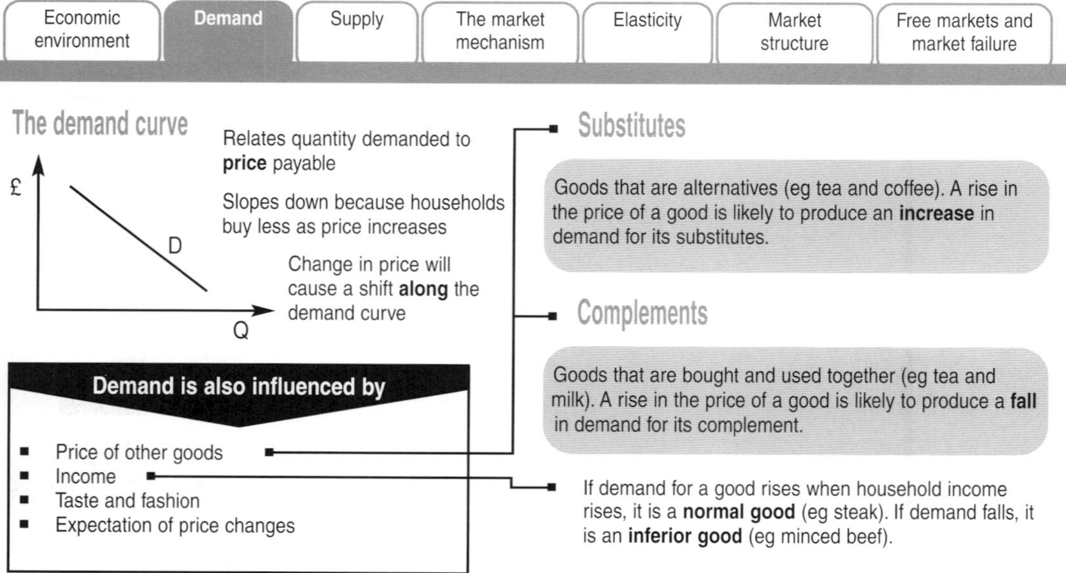
Economic environment
Demand
Supply
The market mechanism
Elasticity
Market structure
Free markets and market failure
The demand curve
£
D
Q
Relates quantity demanded to **price** payable
Slopes down because households buy less as price increases
Change in price will cause a shift **along** the demand curve
Demand is also influenced by
■ Price of other goods
■ Income
■ Taste and fashion
■ Expectation of price changes
Substitutes
Goods that are alternatives (eg tea and coffee). A rise in the price of a good is likely to produce an **increase** in demand for its substitutes.
Complements
Goods that are bought and used together (eg tea and milk). A rise in the price of a good is likely to produce a **fall** in demand for its complement.
If demand for a good rises when household income rises, it is a **normal good** (eg steak). If demand falls, it is an **inferior good** (eg minced beef).

Remember! The demand curve shows how demand responds to a change in price and nothing else! Any change in the other factors that affect demand cause a shift in the position of the demand curve.

A leftward shift may be caused by

- A fall in household income
- A fall in the price of substitutes
- A rise in the price of complements
- A change in taste away from the good
- An expected fall in price

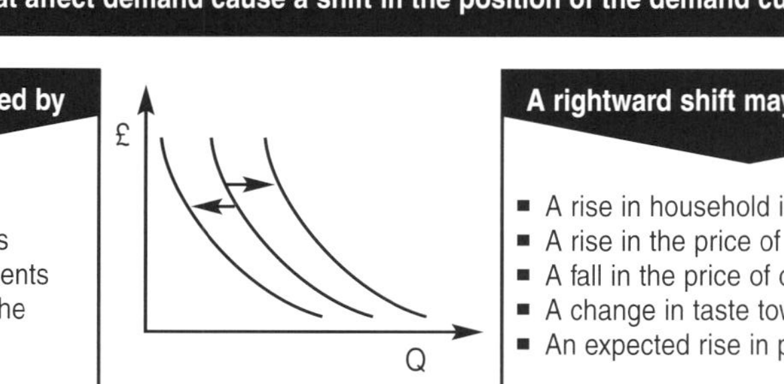

A rightward shift may be caused by

- A rise in household income
- A rise in the price of substitutes
- A fall in the price of complements
- A change in taste towards the good
- An expected rise in price

An expectation of a fall in price will lead consumers to put off their purchases in the hope of benefiting from the lower price later. An expected price rise will lead consumers to buy early and stockpile in order to avoid paying a higher price later.

The supply curve

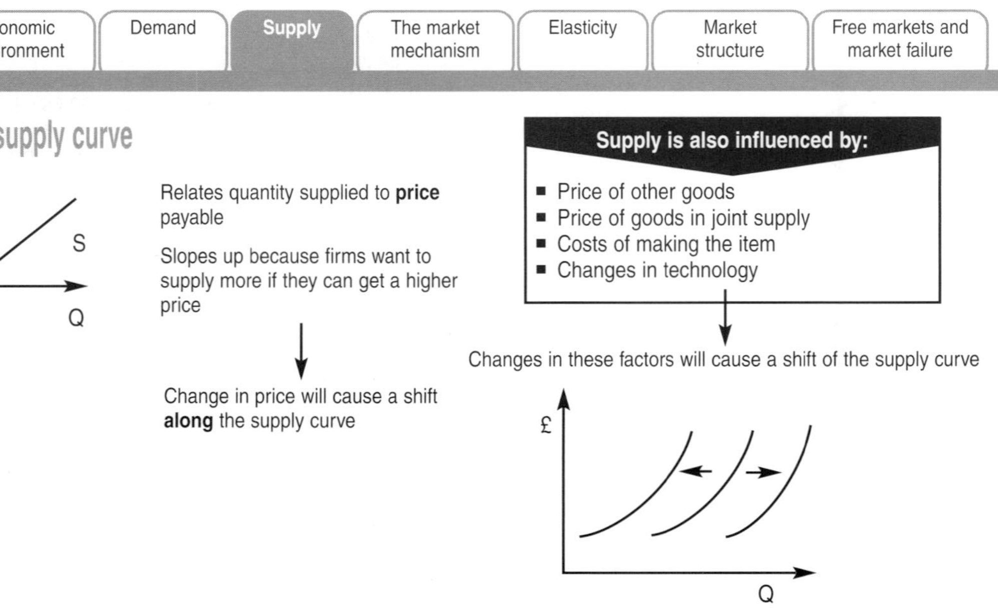

Relates quantity supplied to **price** payable

Slopes up because firms want to supply more if they can get a higher price

Change in price will cause a shift **along** the supply curve

Supply is also influenced by:

- Price of other goods
- Price of goods in joint supply
- Costs of making the item
- Changes in technology

Changes in these factors will cause a shift of the supply curve

The market mechanism

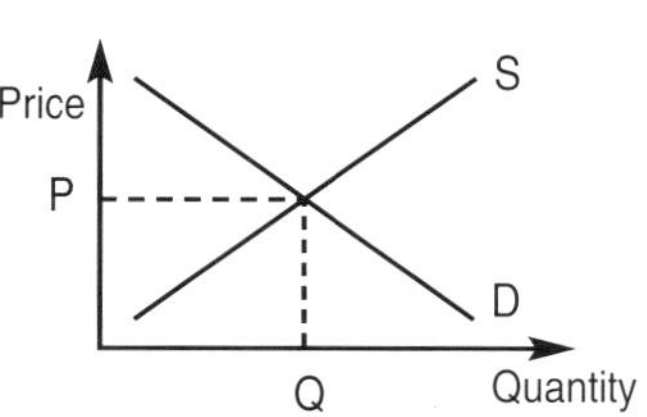

The market mechanism brings supply and demand together at the **equilibrium price** P. This is also the **market clearing price** since quantity Q is both offered and demanded and there is neither surplus nor shortage.

Functions of the market mechanism

- Market prices and their movements act as **signals** to producers, enabling them to produce what is most needed.
- When a firm operates efficiently, responding to market signals and controlling its costs, it receives a **reward** in the form of profit.
- The actions of firms in responding to the profit opportunities **allocate** resources to their best use.

Consumer surplus: some would have paid more than the market price.

Producer surplus: some would have sold at less than the market price.

Price

S

D

Quantity

A shift of the demand or supply curve causes:

- a rise or fall in market price P
- an increase or decrease in quantity supplied Q

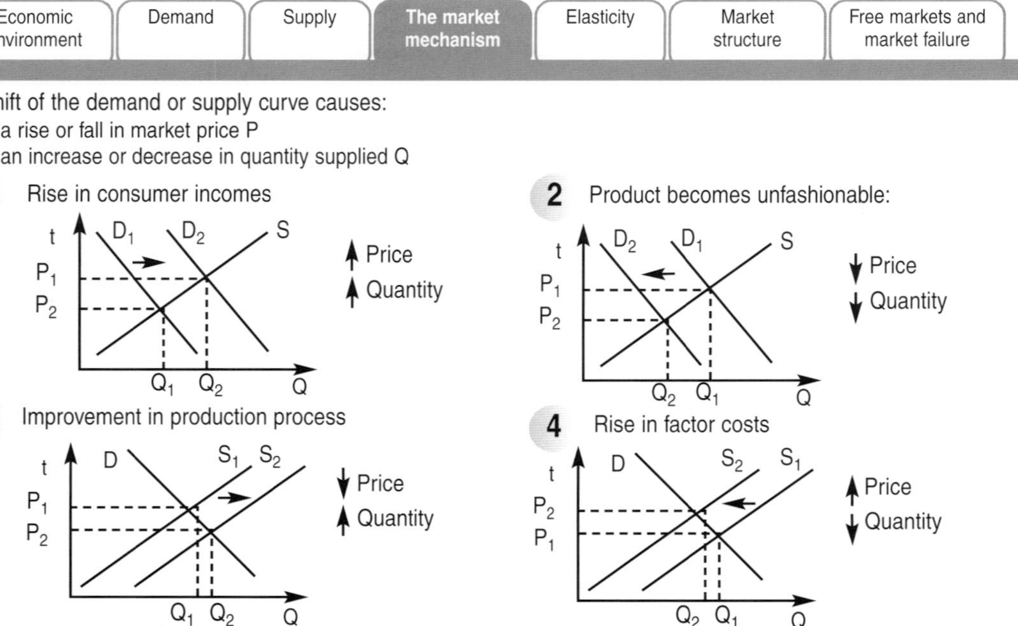

Upward sloping demand curve:

- Giffen goods – basic goods where a rise in price means the necessity of that purchase 'squeezes out' other items
- Veblen goods – goods bought for ostentation

Price regulation

Some governments attempt to overcome market forces by **regulating prices**.

- A **maximum** price might be used to combat inflation or to make basic goods affordable.
- A **minimum** price might be used to secure the incomes of favoured producers, such as farmers.

Price elasticity of demand (PED)

A measure of the change in **demand** for a good in response to a change in its **price**: when demand is **elastic** a small change in price produces a large change in demand. When the demand is inelastic, a large change in price produces only a small change in demand.

$$\text{PED} = \frac{\text{change in quantity demanded as \% of demand}}{\text{change in price as \% of price}} = \frac{\Delta Q}{Q} \times \frac{P}{\Delta P} = \frac{\Delta Q}{\Delta P} \times \frac{P}{Q}$$

P and Q may be values at a **point** or averages over an **arc**.

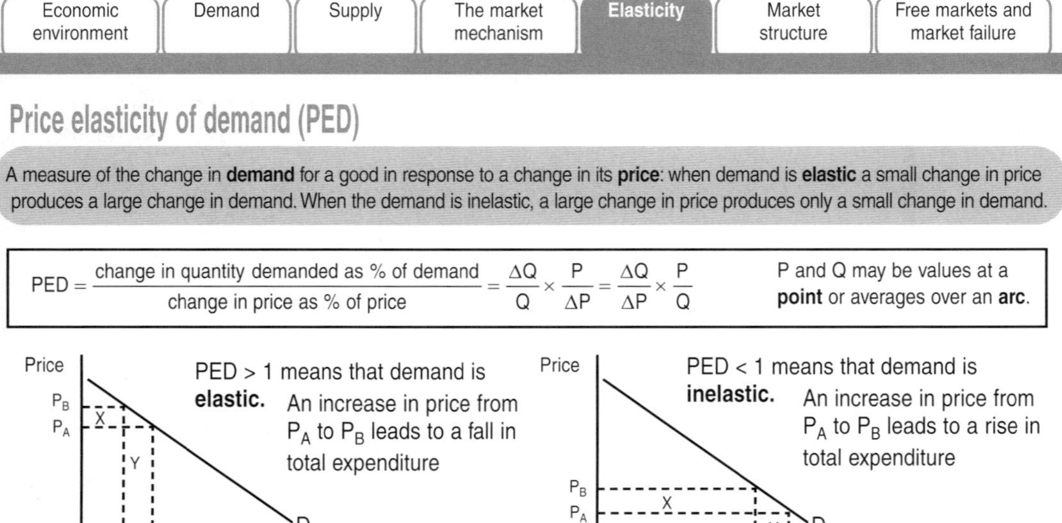

PED > 1 means that demand is **elastic.** An increase in price from P_A to P_B leads to a fall in total expenditure

PED < 1 means that demand is **inelastic.** An increase in price from P_A to P_B leads to a rise in total expenditure

Factors affecting elasticity of supply

- Existence of inventory of all kinds of goods and their perishability
- Ease of adjusting labour inputs up or down
- Barriers to entry make supply inelastic
- Time scale

Factors affecting elasticity of demand

- Availability of substitutes
- Competitors pricing responses
- Necessities = inelastic, luxuries = elastic
- Percentage of income spent on a good – lower = more elastic
- Habit-forming goods = less elastic
- Time scale

Elasticities vary with time

- Households may take a little time to respond to price but demand generally changes quicker than supply.
- During the **market period** only existing inventory and levels of output are available. Supply is **very inelastic**.
- Over the **short run**, quantities can be adjusted by working overtime or short time. Supply is **quite elastic**.
- Over the **long run** plant can be built or shut down. Supply is **very elastic**.

Income elasticity of demand

How demand for a good changes in response to changes in household income

$$\frac{\text{\% change in quantity demanded}}{\text{\% change in household incomes}}$$

- >1 = income elastic → normal good
- <1 = income inelastic → inferior good

Price elasticity of supply

How a supply responds to a change in price

$$\frac{\text{\% change in quantity supplied}}{\text{\% change in price}}$$

- 0 = perfectly inelastic supply → fixed supply
- 1 = unit electricity → proportionate variation of supply with price
- ∝ = perfect elasticity → all is supplied at one price, none at any other price

Cross elasticity of demand

How demand for one good changes in response to a change in the price of another good (assuming no change in price of first good)

$$\frac{\text{\% change in quantity demanded of A}}{\text{\% change in price of B}}$$

- > 0 = positive cross-elasticity → substitutes
- < 0 = negative cross-elasticity → complements
- 0 = unrelated goods

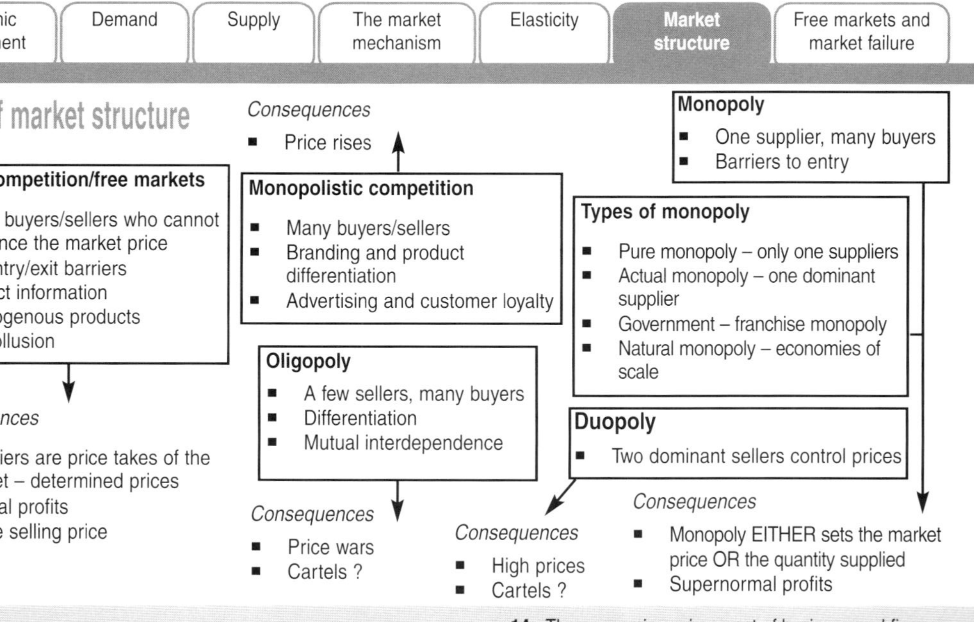
Types of market structure
Perfect competition/free markets
Many buyers/sellers who cannot influence the market price
No entry/exit barriers
Perfect information
Homogenous products
No collusion
Consequences
Suppliers are price takes of the market – determined prices
Normal profits
Single selling price
Monopolistic competition
Many buyers/sellers
Branding and product differentiation
Advertising and customer loyalty
Consequences
Price rises
Oligopoly
A few sellers, many buyers
Differentiation
Mutual interdependence
Consequences
Price wars
Cartels ?
Monopoly
One supplier, many buyers
Barriers to entry
Types of monopoly
Pure monopoly – only one suppliers
Actual monopoly – one dominant supplier
Government – franchise monopoly
Natural monopoly – economies of scale
Duopoly
Two dominant sellers control prices
Consequences
High prices
Cartels ?
Consequences
Monopoly EITHER sets the market price OR the quantity supplied
Supernormal profits

Arguments for free markets

- Rapid adaptations to changing conditions
- Impersonal – price/output result from many individual decisions, not from regulation or central planning
- Efficient allocation of economic resources – suppliers' prices relate to their resource costs; if the market price does not allow profit, ressources will be switched to other products

FAILS

Types of efficiency

- *Social efficiency* takes account of external costs and benefits
- *Allocative efficiency* – goods/services are produced at minimum cost
- *Technical efficiency* – goods/services are produced using minimum amount of resources
- *Productive efficiency* – all goods/services in economy are produced at lowest cost

Assumptions about free markets

- Large number of suppliers with a homogenous product and a small market share each
- Perfect information
- Perfect mobility of factors of production enabling switching
- Free entry to /exit from market

FALSE

MARKET FAILURE

- Free market fails to allocate resources efficiently

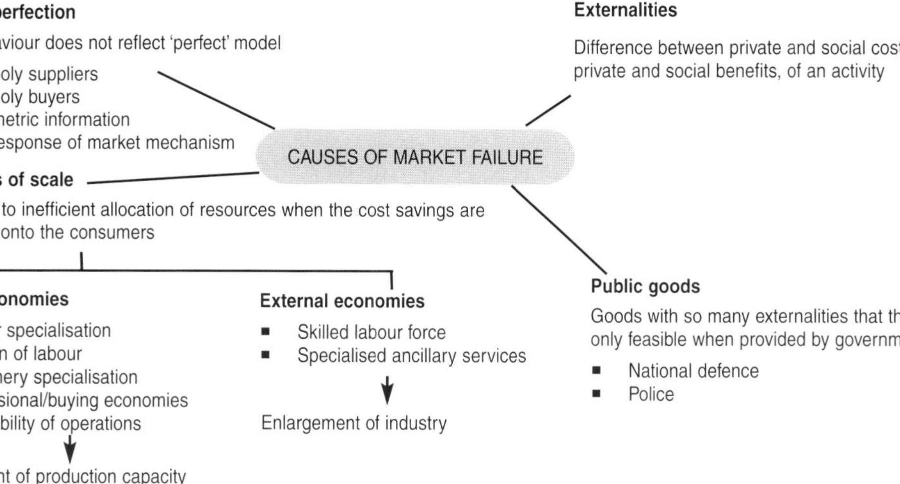
CAUSES OF MARKET FAILURE
Market imperfection
Actual behaviour does not reflect 'perfect' model
■ Monopoly suppliers
■ Monopoly buyers
■ Asymmetric information
■ Slow response of market mechanism
Externalities
Difference between private and social costs or private and social benefits, of an activity
Economies of scale
These lead to inefficient allocation of resources when the cost savings are not passed onto the consumers
Internal economies
■ Labour specialisation
■ Division of labour
■ Machinery specialisation
■ Dimensional/buying economies
■ Indivisibility of operations
Enlargement of production capacity
External economies
■ Skilled labour force
■ Specialised ancillary services
Enlargement of industry
Public goods
Goods with so many externalities that they are only feasible when provided by government
■ National defence
■ Police

15: External regulation of business

Topic List

- Regulation of business
- Regulation of competition
- Regulation of business people
- Sarbanes-Oxley
- Free trade

In this final chapter we cover how governments intervene in markets to address market failures, and to protect the public interest.

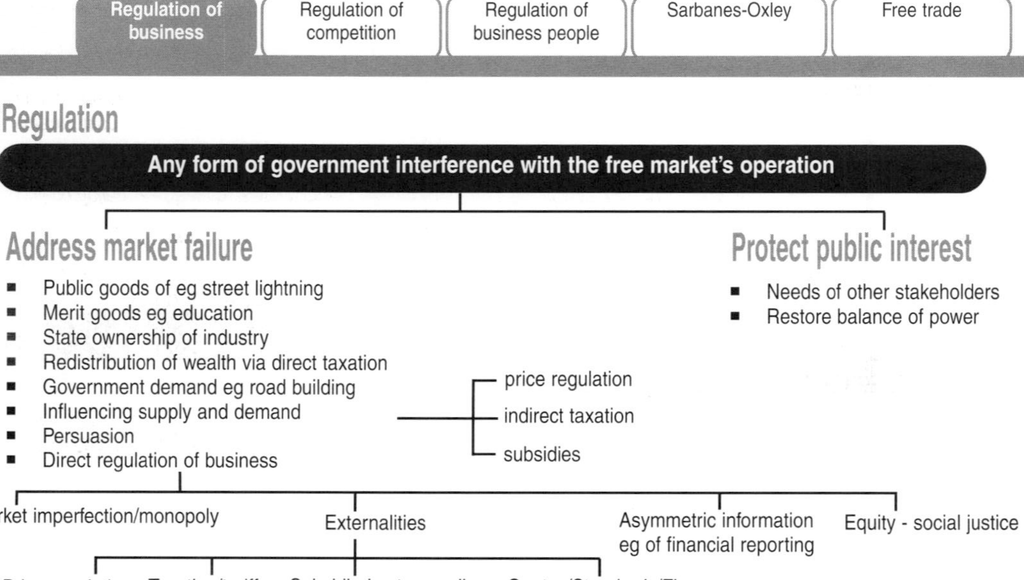

Regulation of business
Regulation of competition
Regulation of business people
Sarbanes-Oxley
Free trade
Regulation
Any form of government interference with the free market's operation
Address market failure
Public goods of eg street lightning
Merit goods eg education
State ownership of industry
Redistribution of wealth via direct taxation
Government demand eg road building
Influencing supply and demand
Persuasion
Direct regulation of business
price regulation
indirect taxation
subsidies
Protect public interest
Needs of other stakeholders
Restore balance of power
Market imperfection/monopoly
Externalities
Asymmetric information eg of financial reporting
Equity - social justice
Price regulation
Taxation/tariffs
Subsidiaries to suppliers
Quotas/Standards/Fines

Forms of business regulation

- Government regulation
- EU regulation

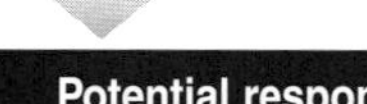

Potential responses of business

- *Entrenchment* = non-response
- *Mere compliance* – cost of compliance passed on to customers
- *Full compliance* – change in behaviour
- *Innovation*: the Porter hypothesis. Environmental regulation triggers discovery/introduction of cleaner technologies and environmental improvements

Efficient regulation: total benefits > total costs

Outcomes of business regulation

- Address market failure
- Change social standing of certain groups
- Implement desires of majority
- Increase diversity
- Deal with irreversibility

Regulatory bodies

- FRC
- FSA
- Environment Agency
- Information Commission
- Office of Fair Trading
- Competition Commission

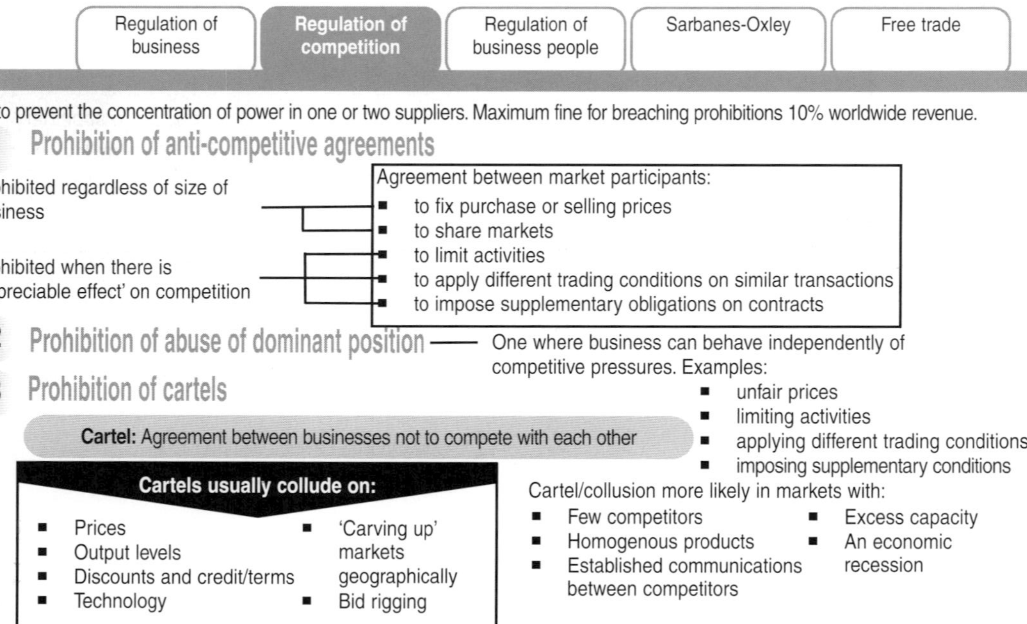
Regulation of business
Regulation of competition
Regulation of business people
Sarbanes-Oxley
Free trade
Aim: to prevent the concentration of power in one or two suppliers. Maximum fine for breaching prohibitions 10% worldwide revenue.
1 Prohibition of anti-competitive agreements
Prohibited regardless of size of business
Prohibited when there is 'appreciable effect' on competition
Agreement between market participants:
to fix purchase or selling prices
to share markets
to limit activities
to apply different trading conditions on similar transactions
to impose supplementary obligations on contracts
2 Prohibition of abuse of dominant position
One where business can behave independently of competitive pressures. Examples:
unfair prices
limiting activities
applying different trading conditions
imposing supplementary conditions
3 Prohibition of cartels
Cartel: Agreement between businesses not to compete with each other
Cartels usually collude on:
Prices
Output levels
Discounts and credit/terms
Technology
'Carving up' markets geographically
Bid rigging
Cartel/collusion more likely in markets with:
Few competitors
Homogenous products
Established communications between competitors
Excess capacity
An economic recession

Competition Commission

The CC may investigate when one firm controls 25% of the market or when a merger involves more than £75m of assets worldwide. It reports to the government. It seeks to promote consumer interests, competition, enterprise and efficiency and tries to balance rewards for innovation and the benefits of scale economies against the disadvantages of monopoly.

Office of Fair Trading

- Powers of investigation
- Imposes penalties
- Third parties can claim damages
- Can make Competition Disqualification orders.

People involved in **listed** and/or **insolvent** companies are regulated with respect to:

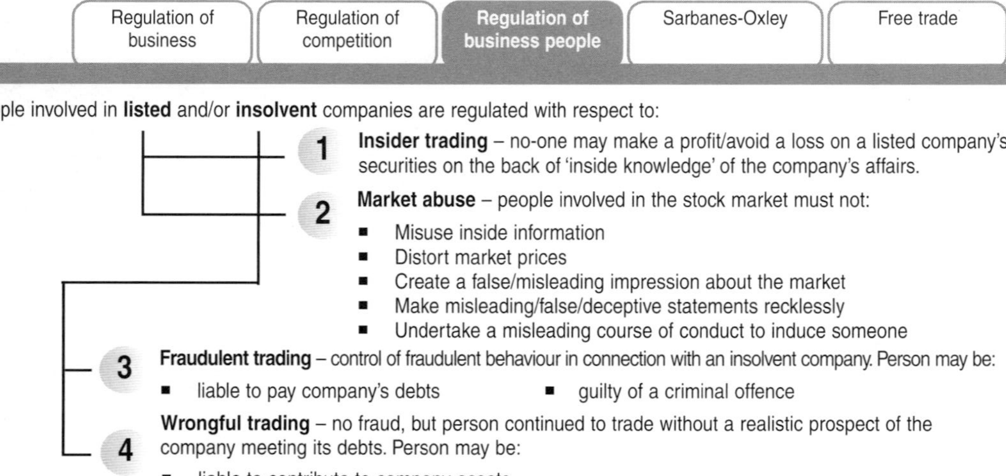

1. **Insider trading** – no-one may make a profit/avoid a loss on a listed company's securities on the back of 'inside knowledge' of the company's affairs.

2. **Market abuse** – people involved in the stock market must not:
   - Misuse inside information
   - Distort market prices
   - Create a false/misleading impression about the market
   - Make misleading/false/deceptive statements recklessly
   - Undertake a misleading course of conduct to induce someone

3. **Fraudulent trading** – control of fraudulent behaviour in connection with an insolvent company. Person may be:
   - liable to pay company's debts
   - guilty of a criminal offence

4. **Wrongful trading** – no fraud, but person continued to trade without a realistic prospect of the company meeting its debts. Person may be:
   - liable to contribute to company assets

Disqualification of directors

Director may be disqualified from acting as a director for:

- Insider trading, wrongful and fraudulent trading
- Being the director of an insolvent company
- Being unfit to act
- Being a threat to the public interest

Sarbanes-Oxley Act

The Sarbanes-Oxley Act was a response to the collapse of Enron, one of America's biggest companies. The Act is prescriptive, impacting on disclosures, audits, ethics and directors' share trading.

Weaknesses at Enron

- Lack of transparency in financial statements
- Non-executive directors weak
- Lack of external audit scrutiny
- Directors' use of inside information
- Dishonesty and law-breaking

Application of the Act

To companies whose securities are listed in the US, and therefore to their subsidiaries wherever located.

Corporate responsibility

Chief executive/chief finance officer certify:

- Appropriateness of financial statements
- Financial statement fairly reflect operations and financial conditions.

If financial statement have to be restated, CE/CFO forfeit their bonuses.

Audit committees

Every US listed company should have an audit committee consisting of independent directors, with member(s) with financial expertise. Audit committee should be responsible for:

- Appointment, compensation and oversight of auditors
- Discussing key accounting policies with auditors
- Setting up complaints mechanisms

Whistleblowing

Employees/auditors are granted whistleblowing protection if they disclose private employer information to parties involved in a fraud claim.

Internal control reports

Annual financial statement must contain internal control reports that:

- State management responsibility for control structure/financial reporting procedures
- Assess effectiveness of control structure/financial reporting procedures (with audit report)
- State whether code of conduct for senior financial officers has been adopted

Off-balance sheet transactions

There should be appropriate disclosure of material off-balance sheet transactions.

Trade, advantage and specialisation

A country has an **absolute advantage** in the production of a good if it can produce it at lower cost than other countries. It has a **comparative advantage** if it can product it at lower **opportunity cost**, that is, at lower cost in terms of production of other goods foregone. This means that total global output will be maximised if countries specialise and trade.

Globalisation

Globalisation is the process whereby first markets and then supply become organised on a global scale. Tastes and preferences become common across country borders. Manufacturing is organised in several countries and components are sourced world-wide. Other global drivers include the existence of international financial facilities, cultural similarities between nations, international commodity markets and the development of free trade agreements.

Advantages of free international trade

- ✓ Efficient resource allocation
- ✓ Equalise surpluses/deficits of resources
- ✓ Increased competition
- ✓ Large markets = economies of scale
- ✓ Build political links

Protectionism

Governments resort to protectionism in order to preserve employment in individual industries, to support their country's balance of payments or to guard strategically important assets.

- **Tariffs** are taxes on imports. They raise revenue for governments; the extra cost is passed on via higher prices, thus discouraging purchases.
- **Non-tariff barriers** include quotas, embargoes and import licences; minimum local content rules; minimum prices; subsidies for domestic producers and currency restrictions.
- **Covert barriers** are operated to hamper imports and include inspection procedures; packaging and labelling requirements; toleration of anti-competitive practices among home producers and distribution obstacles.

Regional trade organisations have promoted free trade within their areas.

A free trade area has:	A customs union adds:	A common market adds:
Free movement of goods and services	Common external tariffs	Free movement of the factors of production

Arguments for protection

- **Employment protection**: cheap imports from low wage countries mean domestic industries cannot compete. Business failure and unemployment ensue.
- **Balance of payments**: imports must be financed or the exchange rate will be driven down (see Chapter 19). Restricting imports reduces the pressure.
- **Infant industries**: less developed countries need to assist their developing industries to become established.
- **Unfair trade practices**: exporters may sell at less than cost ('dumping') to gain a foothold; governments may subsidise exports.
- **Revenue**: tariffs raise revenue painlessly.
- **Strategic industries**: some industries (defence, agriculture) are favoured for strategic reasons.

Arguments against protection

- **Reduction in welfare**: protection reduces global trade and hence global production.
- **Inefficiency**: domestic industries become inefficient through lack of competition. Also, declining industries linger and new ones are hampered.
- **Higher prices**: cheap imports reduce the cost of living.
- **Retaliation**: retaliatory response by other countries is likely to harm the domestic economy.

European Union

The European Union (EU) combines a free trade area with a customs union and a common market. The aim is complete freedom of trade, including free movement of capital and labour and no national preference in the award of public sector contracts. However, barriers still exist in the form of different tax systems, infrastructure, skill levels and prosperity.

The **European Economic Area** links the EU to Norway and Iceland.

North American Free Trade Agreement

The North American Free Trade Agreement links Mexico, the USA and Canada in a free trade area.

Aims of the World Trade Organisation

- Reduce barriers to free trade
- Eliminate discrimination in trade
- Deter protectionist measures

Notes

Notes

Notes